No Time for House Plants

NO TIME FOR HOUSE PLANTS

A Busy Person's Guide to Indoor Gardening

By Jerry Minnich

Text illustrations by Dian W. Hjertman

University of Oklahoma Press : Norman

By Jerry Minnich

A Wisconsin Garden Guide (Madison, 1975)
The Earthworm Book (Emmaus, Pa., 1977)
No Time for House Plants (Norman, 1979)

Library of Congress Cataloging in Publication Data

Minnich, Jerry.
    No time for house plants.

    Bibliography: p. 132
    Includes index.
    1. House plants.   2. Indoor gardening.
I. Title.
SB419.M63   635.9'65   78–58102
ISBN 0–8061–1499–1

For my mother,
Helen Memory Wild

Contents

Preface

This book is a guide to raising house plants for people who have no time to raise house plants.

Many of us—single people, working couples, harassed mothers, college students, people who travel frequently, anyone whose daily living pattern leaves precious little time for indoor gardening—would enjoy the beauty and companionship of bright, green and flowering house plants, especially through the drab winter months. Past failures, however, have led us to believe that we cannot raise indoor plants without giving them more time and attention than we can provide. Beautiful gift plants may have quickly withered and perished. The bright little ivy, bought on impulse at the supermarket, may never have made it past childhood on the kitchen windowsill. Then the books and articles written by house plant experts present, in loving and extended detail, the special methods *they* use to achieve success—and it seems as though house plant growing must be a consuming hobby if it is to produce gratifying results.

Not so! The gift plant you received probably would not have survived in your dry home atmosphere, no matter how much attention it received. The first secret of house plant success is in choosing the right plants in the beginning, and gift plants from the florist are very often the wrong plants entirely for home conditions. The little ivy was perhaps given too little sun, or an atmosphere much too warm and dry, or too much water, or too little growing room. Secret number two is in giving each plant the very best conditions that your home can offer. The right plant, given the right conditions, will thrive despite your frequent inattention.

This book is meant not only for busy people but also for busy people who have no long or extensive experience in growing house plants. The green-thumb aficionado with a collection of two hundred thriving exotic specimens will see at a glance that there are no revolutionary breakthroughs revealed here, no closely guarded secrets unveiled, but simply a collection of solid and practical information, trimmed of excess detail and shaped for a single purpose: *to help you to achieve house plant success without really working at it.*

Last, we have created this book to be a pleasant companion in itself, one that can provide a pleasant few hours of reading and also one to which you may refer time and time again for the answers to many questions about your house plants. It might even be your traveling companion, for it will serve as a guide to your choosing plant varieties at the florist shop or garden center. However it is used, I would hope that this volume, modest in both size and scope, will lead you to success with house plants and eventually to a love for them. Should that happen, it will have more than achieved its purpose.

Ready to grow house plants without working at it? Then let's go!

The following symbols are used throughout to indicate the temperature preference, light needs, soil moisture and humidity needs, and best window locations for each plant described:

Temperature Preference

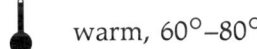　warm, 60°–80°

　moderate, 50°–70°

　　cool, 45°–60°

Light Needs

　　full sun

　　tolerates some direct sun

　　bright spot with no direct sun

　　tolerates continuous shade

Soil Moisture and Humidity Needs

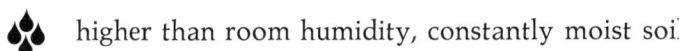　higher than room humidity, constantly moist soil

　moderate humidity and soil moisture

　　tolerates dry conditions

Best Window Location

　　north

　　south or west

　　east

Acknowledgments

Many authors pay well-deserved tribute to their editors, who guide their efforts in so many ways, correcting misspellings, suggesting ways to improve structure and syntax, bridling overly exuberant statements, catching errors of fact, pruning redundancies, suggesting needed additions, making inconsistencies properly consistent, casting out useless sentences and paragraphs, and in general making the author's work intelligible to others. Behind every successful author is a competent and long-suffering editor.

My debt is great, indeed, for I have not one editor to thank, or even two or three, but fully nine, and doubtless some more of whom I have remained unaware.

The foregoing statement requires a little explanation, which will lead into a short history of this book's creation. It all began in 1975 when some university press publishers were casting about for a project on which to focus the 1977 annual meeting of the Association of American University Presses. Hilary Marshall, of the University of Toronto Press, had the idea of giving an identical book manuscript to each of five university presses, well in advance of the meeting, and asking that each edit the manuscript and carry out all plans of publication right up to the point of manufacturing the book. At the annual meeting, then, all university press people could examine the papers of the five cooperating presses, compare and contrast their methods and procedures, and perhaps learn something more about book publishing.

At the time, I was thinking seriously about writing a book on house plants for busy people. I mentioned this to Hilary at New York's La Guardia Airport, while we both were waiting for homeward flights, and by the next week the concept was given wheels: *No Time for House Plants* was to be the association's model manuscript.

I worked on the book throughout the winter and spring of 1975–76, traveling to Pennsylvania and Washington, D.C. to carry out some research, and finally presented the completed manuscript to the five university presses in early summer. For the next year all five presses expended untold hours of work to produce a complete set of papers which described in full the publishing procedures each used. These papers were duplicated, collated, and bound into a book, called *One Book/Five Ways*, which was distributed at the 1977 annual meeting. It was received with such enthusiasm that another publisher, William Kaufmann, Inc., offered to publish it as an educational volume for editors, publishers, and authors. It was so published in 1978.

Where, then, can I begin to acknowledge the help I have received in the preparation of this book? Perhaps with my mother, who first suggested—at the time I was writing a book about earthworms—that I write a book on a sensible topic, like house plants. Certainly, my debt is great to the editors and other staff members of those five cooperating presses. At the MIT Press, I appreciated working with Nancy Greenhouse, Robin Cruise, and designer Mario Furtado. At North Carolina, I thank Malcolm MacDonald, Gwen Duffy, Barbara Reitt, Ann Sulkin, Marjorie Fowler, and, especially, designer Joyce Kachergis, whose early enthusiasm and long devotion to the project virtually assured its success. At Toronto, of course, there was the inspiring Hilary Marshall as well as the indefatigable Agatha Q. Sigglesthwaite. At Texas, Carolyn Cates Wylie lent her fine editorial hand to complement Rich Hendel's enthusiastic design. And at the University of Chicago Press, I admired the fully professional talents of Catharine Seybold and Kimberly Wiar, and of designer Cameron Poulter.

There are others. At the New York office of the Association of American University Presses, Jack Putnam, Carol Franz, Jerry Lewis, Rita Black, and Alice Baer all gave of their considerable energies and talents in coordinating a most difficult project.

My wife, Nancy, not only gave of her time in proofreading and advising me throughout the preparation of the manuscript, but also suffered quite cheerfully as I struggled for months with Latin plant names.

Then, I must thank all of the people at the University of Oklahoma Press who, first, offered to publish the book "for real," and then did so with their customary verve and professionalism.

There are more to thank—Jess Bell of Stanford University Press and Chandler Grannis of *Publishers Weekly*, whose enthusiasm for the project was both inspiring and reassuring —and dozens more, some of whom, as I say, I am still unaware. All had a part in bringing forth this modest volume, the appearance of which I hope will, in some small way, justify their generosity of talent and spirit.

Jerry Minnich

Madison, Wisconsin
August 18, 1978

No Time for House Plants

 The Secrets of No-Time House Plant Success

When there is no time to dote on house plants, the secrets for success are but three, and they are simple:

1. Choose plants that are tolerant of varying conditions, ones that are willing to take the abuse you can dish out.

2. Give them the best growing conditions your home can offer.

3. Learn the tricks that will enable you to maintain them with an absolute minimum of care.

The first of these rules is not difficult to follow, since more than a hundred plants and plant groups, comprising several thousand individual varieties, are recommended in this book. Included are my three dozen "best bets" for no-time gardeners—thirty-six plants that I consider to be the most tolerant and easy to maintain of all. Even if you limit your plant selections to this group, you can build an impressive small collection that includes some unusual varieties. But you may feel free to roam farther than the thirty-six "best bets," since none of the plants recommended in this book is really difficult to grow. Any that might present something of a challenge is so indicated.

The second rule is similarly simple to follow, since the environmental conditions required for each plant are given with the plant's listing in the following chapters. After you have chosen plants that will grow in your home, you should determine *what particular spot* is best for each plant you have selected. A little time in making these decisions will be repaid many times over in savings of your time.

The third rule—learning the tricks that will help your plants to take care of themselves—is less clear-cut. I have suggested some such tricks in these pages, including preventive pruning, and ways in which to use watering and lighting to control plant growth. The last thing the no-work gardener wants is a roomful of plants in rank growth, crying out for pruning, staking, tying, and plant food. There are ways to slow the growth of plants and still keep them in good health. I have outlined some of them in Chapter 2; you will doubtless come across others as you experiment with your own house plants and discuss their care with other indoor gardeners.

In order to understand the recommendations in this book, you should have at least a skeletal understanding of a plant's basic needs, as dictated by its environmental history. The first thing to remember is that, in nature, a true *house* plant does not exist, unless you choose to count those few varieties that have found happiness in the entrances to caves or in the hollows of trees. Every plant in your home has been removed from an environment to which it has become adapted over countless centuries of evolution. The Jerusalem cherry that you bring home from the supermarket at Christmas, for instance, comes from Madeira, off the northwest coast of Africa, where it has become used to mild temperatures and sunny skies. The vigorous Wandering Jew in your hanging basket hails from Central or South America, where it has thrived for thousands of years in a warmer climate. African violets were brought from the moist and warm forest floors of that continent, where they found shelter in the shade of trees. The tough cast-iron plant is a native of China's temperate climate, where it learned to survive under a wide range of weather conditions. Bromeliads in nature grow in the crotches of tropical trees. Aralia, boxwood, and other Japanese evergreen shrubs prefer the cool conditions of their native environments.

Each plant, in fact, has had over thousands of years to become adapted to conditions of soil, climate, and light that you will not be able to duplicate exactly. Fortunately all plants also have a certain tolerance to these conditions. Some have more tolerance than others, however, and these more tolerant plants are the ones I have chosen for this book.

Before growing any plant you should take some time to understand its individual needs, be fairly certain that you can offer them, and then choose the best spot in your home for that particular plant. In this way you will greatly increase your chances for success, and your plants will be able to thrive with little of your personal attention.

If you always keep in mind the first two rules—wise plant selection and the heeding of each plant's needs—then there is no reason why you cannot raise as many as two dozen house plants by spending no more than ten minutes with them every other day and perhaps a half-hour every two weeks in pruning, spraying, cleaning the leaves of large-leafed varieties, and fertilizing. Once or twice a year you might spend a pleasant afternoon in repotting a few favorites or in some major pruning. You can, of course, spend more time in fussing if you enjoy it and have the time, but it is really not necessary. This book will give you the information you need to allow your plants to take care of themselves fairly well, even when you are away from home for two weeks or more.

WHEN THERE'S NO TIME FOR HOUSE PLANTS

Part of the secret in growing beautiful house plants, when you have no time for house plants, lies in your basic approach to the necessary chores.

How, you may ask, am I going to mist all these plants, keep them watered and fertilized, prune and train them, repot them, and fight insects and disease, when I really don't have the time or would rather be doing something else?

Part of the answer is in what I call the "bit-and-snatch" method of house plant care. You take just a bit of time here, snatch a moment there, during times when you aren't really doing anything else. There are many times like this in the daily life of even the busiest people. For example, in the two minutes it takes for the coffee to perk or the pot to boil, you could mist a dozen plants. In the minute it takes for the eggs to fry, you could pick off all the yellowing leaves from a Jerusalem cherry plant. While waiting three minutes to get into the bathroom, you could tie up those new shoots of the grape ivy. Nearly all the chores necessary to keep your house plants thriving are little ones. Work them into your daily routine, and you will soon see that they take no extra time at all, because you will be spending no time in "tending to the house plants."

Look for other time-savers. When I suggest using rainwater for house plants, I do not ask that you make a big point of capturing rainwater. Work it into your daily routine. Keep a barrel or a bucket in the back yard, and keep two large jars for transporting the rainwater indoors. If there happens to be water in the barrel as you are coming in the back door, take ten seconds to scoop up a jarful and bring it in with you. When you go back out, take an empty jar and place it behind the barrel. Don't make a special trip for the purpose.

When you are going to take a shower, take a plant or two with you, so that they can gain the benefits of the bathroom humidity for a few hours. Carry them back to their permanent places later in the day or even the following day— any time that you happen to be going from the bathroom to the room where the plant lives. Again, don't make a special trip, but do work it into your daily routine.

Important, also, is to go slowly in acquiring plants. Get to know a plant well before buying another. If any plant does not seem to be responding well to its new home, it might take a bit of time for you to discover the reason. The location might be wrong, or you might be giving it too much water or too much sun—or too little of either. It takes very little time to do a little research and experimentation to help one plant become oriented; it is quite another matter when you are doing the same for five or six. Build your house plant collection gradually, if you do not want a joy to become a burden.

Another time-saver is to keep all of your plants having similar requirements in one general area of the house or apartment, so that you can water and mist them as a group. Your hardy *Aspidistra* and that dusty snake plant can find happiness nearly anywhere, and they wouldn't miss not being watered for a week or not being cleaned or misted for months at a time. But do group your other plants in locations that best serve the needs of the group. Your English ivy, spider plant, and wandering Jew can tolerate conditions on the semi-dry side; do not, then, keep them with moisture lovers such as *Dieffenbachia* and *Scindapsus*. You will find it quicker to water plants when they are so grouped, and you will also have an easier time in remembering which are moisture lovers. Similarly, do not keep plants that do not like to be misted, such as your African violet, with those that love mist.

Of course, you will also have to keep in mind other requirements of each plant, including its need for light and temperature preference. You should take some time in the beginning in grouping your plants for ease in maintenance. This will be time well spent, since it will save your time forever after. And when selecting a new plant for your collection, choose one that will fit into one of the groups you have already established. If you do, the plant will take no more of your time.

This matter of choosing the right plants is particularly important in the no-time method. You probably have enough to worry about without rubbing your hands over an exotic fern that threatens to brown out totally unless its unreasonable demands for humidity are constantly met. Are you willing to sit up with a sick begonia whose blossoms drop the minute they are formed? Will you feel increasingly guilty as your pothos refuses to eat, growing paler by the day? Of course not! One rule of no-time house plant growing, in my book, is: *If a plant gives you more trouble than it is worth, get rid of it.* Your Aunt Ethel would probably love to nurse the fern back to health. The begonia might be better suited to the outside. And the pothos would doubtless be far happier in the hands of one of your house plant doting friends or even in the compost heap, where it eventually can help to make a tomato grow at least. Don't be afraid to throw out a house plant. You don't need an assertiveness training course to deal ruthlessly with an ingrate plant.

Another sensible rule, passed on to me by a friend in an advertising agency, is: Never spend more than fifteen dollars for a house plant. I would reduce that figure to ten dollars, or even to seven-fifty. If you spend a lot of money for a plant, you are going to feel strongly obligated to make it succeed— often at a cost in time that you wouldn't pay, were the plant less of an investment. What profit is there in putting in ten hours of your time on a twenty-dollar *Calathea*, when only the most experienced of growers can succeed with this ungrateful plant in any case?

Then which plants should you choose? How can you know which will reward you with carefree growth, vibrant health, and genuine beauty? One clue is to observe carefully the plants in other people's homes. If you see an impressive look-ing plant you really like, ask about it. Particularly if the owner does not have a renowned green thumb, ask if he or she has had much trouble with this plant. After a cursory discussion in which you properly express your admiration for the plant and for the host's skill in growing it, you will probably be offered a cutting. If not, then hint about being offered one. You will probably receive several cuttings, which you can root in sand or water, thereby obtaining a desirable house plant at absolutely no cost. You might even see the same plant at your local shop and pick up an established specimen for a few dollars.

To make things even easier, however, I have chosen thirty-six plants, which I consider to be the best bets of all. Following is a list of those three dozen, which together offer a wide range of species to suit nearly any taste. In this list are foliage plants and flowering plants, climbers and treelike plants, plants for hanging baskets and for large tubs. If you have no plants now but would like to start a collection, go to your favorite shop and, choosing from among these, establish a group of perhaps a half-dozen. Before you make your final selections, check carefully the proper conditions that each requires and be fairly certain that your home can offer them. Then find the best spot in your home for each plant. If, after doing this, you encounter continuing problems with any plant, get rid of it and buy another of a different species. Build your collection slowly, success upon success, keeping only those plants that respond well to the conditions you can offer.

THREE DOZEN EASY-TO-GROW PLANTS FOR NO-TIME GARDENERS

Aloe variegata
Amaryllis
Aralia *(Fatsia japonica)*
Arrowhead
Asparagus fern
Aspidistra
Baby's tears
Billbergia nutans (a bromeliad)
Break fern
Cactus (most species)
Chinese evergreen
Christmas cactus
Coleus
Crown of thorns
Dracaena godseffiana 'Florida Beauty'
Echeveria
English ivy
Fatshedra lizei

Grape ivy
Jade plant
Lithops
Mistletoe fig
Pilea
Poinsettia
Rubber plant
Screw pine
Snake plant
Spathe flower
Spider plant
Strawberry geranium
Swedish ivy
Umbrella tree
Velvet plant
Vulcan plant
Wandering Jew
Wax ivy

When you get to the shop, you will find that there is more than one variety or subspecies of many of these plants. You might find a half-dozen kinds of wandering Jew and as many or more variations on English ivy. The number and variety of house plants are, in fact, staggering. For every combination of conditions your home can offer, there are hundreds or even thousands of suitable house plants offering a virtually limitless selection of sizes, forms, colors, patterns, textures, growth patterns, and flowering habits. You have only to survey the conditions you can offer and then make your selections, within those limits, to suit your own tastes.

The house plants I have selected for inclusion in this book are only representative of their far greater numbers. I have included nearly all of the most common plants, and I have tried to avoid those difficult to grow. All the old favorites are here, as well as some newer varieties and unusual plants that can add zest to your collection.

In Chapters 3 and 4 (on foliage plants and flowering plants), the plants are listed alphabetically by their common names, followed by their scientific (Latin) names. The scientific name comprises both the generic name and the specific epithet. For example, the scientific name for the common boxwood is *Buxus* (the genus) *sempervirens* (the species). After a genus name is introduced, it is thereafter abbreviated. Thus *Buxus sempervirens*, if mentioned again soon after, becomes *B. sempervirens*. Last, there may be a third part to the scientific name, which designates a further subdivision, usually called a subspecies or variety. The popular Japanese boxwood, for example, is *B. microphylla japonica*.

Although I prefer to maintain an informal tone in these pages, by using common names whenever possible, the scientific nomenclature has obvious benefits. Many species are known by different common names in different parts of the country; different species of a genus are often called by a single common name; and a single common name may be applied even to species of completely different genera. There are times, then, when the only way to avoid confusion is to use the scientific name.

For each plant listed you will find symbols that indicate its individual preferences for growing temperature, light, soil moisture and air humidity, and window placement. Please remember that these are rough guides and not inflexible demands. Many plants have a surprisingly wide range of tolerance and will thrive in a variety of conditions. Many of the plants I recommend for an east window will do just as well in a shaded south or a west location. Do not hesitate to try a plant of your liking simply because you cannot provide its exact needs—but neither should you attempt a plant if you can provide none of them. Temperature and humidity are perhaps most critical, since it is not difficult to control the other conditions—light, watering, and window placement. Above all, do not be afraid to experiment. Any plant might do better than you expect it to.

WHERE TO BUY HOUSE PLANTS

The best place to buy a house plant is from someone who

grows house plants. The grower will know the plants well, and you will be able to rely on his or her advice. If there is no grower in your community, the next best source is your local house plant store, flower shop, or nursery center. Whichever you choose, talk to the owner or manager about house plants. Ask for precise identification of a plant that interests you. Ask for specifications of the plant's needs for light, soil, temperature, and humidity. Ask how large the plant is likely to become and whether or not it produces flowers—even if you already know the answers to these questions. If it becomes apparent that the person to whom you're talking doesn't know very much about the plant, or about house plants in general, then ask to talk to someone who can answer your questions in greater detail, or seek another source.

Plants found in supermarkets and discount houses are usually not bad, although many you see flowering in the store may have been grown quickly and forced into bloom (or tender growth) under ideal greenhouse conditions that you cannot hope to match in your home. Larger plants offered at bargain prices may be severely underrooted. However, most plants offered by these sources are likely to be common varieties that are quite tolerant of adverse conditions. It is hard to go wrong with grape ivy or a snake plant.

Plants stored outside at garden centers or in shopping centers may carry insects or disease, particularly if they are resting close to flats of outdoor vegetable or flower seedlings. Examine them closely before purchasing, and isolate them for one or two weeks at home before putting them with other house plants.

Wherever you buy your plants, look for young and sturdy specimens with rich color and a generally healthy appearance. Examine particularly carefully large and mature plants that carry high price tags. These may have been growing for too long a time under ideal greenhouse conditions. Sometimes you will have better luck with a younger plant, and you will have the added pleasure of bringing it to maturity in your own home.

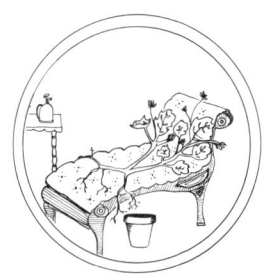

 Understanding House Plants

Every plant has its own preferences and requirements for soil type, light, temperature, ventilation, humidity, and several other factors that are within our power to control or at least to mitigate. It will be well worth your while to gain some understanding of these factors, because this basic knowledge will enable you to avoid much work later on while achieving routine success in growing plants.

In addition to understanding these basic needs, you will want to know something about pots and other containers, repotting plants, propagation, and a few other matters that, while not vital to routine success, will help you to gain further enjoyment in raising better plants.

THE BASIC HOUSE PLANT

The major difference between a house plant and an outdoor plant is that of location. All house plants could live and flourish outdoors in the proper climate. All are derived from forebears that lived, reproduced, and died outdoors, whether it was on a forest floor in central Europe or in the bough of a tree in a South American rain forest. Over many centuries of adaptation and evolution each plant species embraced those characteristics that enabled it to survive; even today every house plant carries within its genetic structure the characteristics of its distant progenitors. Thus the *Maranta* might lose some of its leaves each autumn, even though autumn's weather does not come to the top of the bookshelf where the plant rests. And a cactus, no matter how long we have been feeding and watering it with unfailing regularity, will continue to hoard food and water within its swollen stems. In plants old habits might recede, but they are never forgotten.

At no time are these innate plant characteristics more noticeable than during the autumn and winter, when many plants—particularly those from temperate regions—enter a period of rest or dormancy. Then new growth ceases and the plant takes on a listless and washed-out appearance. Other plants, including many of tropical origin, will maintain their bright appearance but will stop growing completely for several months each year, emulating the natural rest periods of their forebears.

Of course, indoor plants will respond to reduced light conditions of the winter months, and it is difficult to separate this environmental factor from a plant's genetic tendencies. In any case, however, you will do well to watch for these signs of dormancy and respond to each plant's needs at that time. When any plant enters a dormant or rest period, water should be reduced and fertilizer withheld completely, until new growth once again begins, usually in the late winter or early spring. At that time water the plant freely and resume its normal doses of fertilizer in order to encourage new growth. By your proper treatment of the plant at this time you will emulate the advent of spring, working with the plant in carrying out its rhythmic cycles.

With some plants, especially those of tropical origin, you can escape any natural rest period by providing the plant with artificial light and good humidity over the winter months. Whether this forcing of a plant to maximum growth is harmful or not is a matter of debate. In any case it is best done in a terrarium, where conditions can be maintained easily at any time of the year.

Some plants also are naturally short-lived and will last

15

no more than a year or two in your home despite your careful attention, because their genetic structure dictates a finite life span. Garden annuals, for instance, will germinate, grow to maturity, flower, produce seeds, and die, all in as little as six months. For this reason very few annuals are selected as house plants. Although a few short-lived plants are cultivated indoors for their unusual characteristics, such as the sensitive plant, which is easily grown from seed, the house plants that we have cultivated over the generations are most often those that will give years of pleasure. Some house plants, in fact, live to be literally hundreds of years old.

Still other house plants are attractive when young but grow ungainly or otherwise unattractive when they approach maturity. The only plants of this kind I have chosen for inclusion in this book are those that are very easy to propagate from cuttings, so that the parent plant may be discarded after a year or two and replaced by its children.

From the hundreds of thousands of plant species in the world, those traditionally cultivated as house plants are the relatively few that have shown a wide tolerance to conditions of heat, light, moisture, humidity, and ventilation—in other words, those that can withstand a human environment. They are both attractive to the eye and tough. Still, if we are looking for success with house plants—and particularly success without working hard at it—then we should spend some time to learn the characteristics of each plant, recognizing its individual needs and fulfilling them to the best of our abilities.

HOW A PLANT FEEDS

A plant manufactures nearly all of its food by itself—and not from the "plant food" you buy for it. Commercial plant food is no more than a combination of certain chemicals (sometimes in an organic base) that are essential to the plant's basic functioning, much as vitamins are essential to human nutrition. But the bulk of a plant's food—the sugar it uses for energy and growth—is manufactured by the plant itself. In the presence of light the leaves or other green parts of the plant draw carbon dioxide from the air and water from the roots, converting these into sugar that is then used for energy production or stored for future use.

During this sugar manufacturing process, known as photo-synthesis, several other things happen within the plant. While carbon dioxide is absorbed, oxygen is released from the pores of the leaf surface. (Plants produce—at least initially—not only all of the world's food but most of its atmospheric oxygen as well.) During darkness the process is reversed; some of the atmosphere's oxygen is recaptured by the plant and used to convert stored sugar to energy for growth. Generally a plant manufactures growth food during the day and does its actual growing at night.

Often the plant converts its newly manufactured sugar to starch and stores it, reconverting it to sugar as the need arises. Although the starch can be stored in almost any area of the plant, certain plants have developed specialized storage areas just for this purpose. Cacti and succulents have enlarged stems and leaves for the greatest above-ground storage capacity of any house plant, while others have developed underground storage apparatuses for this purpose, including bulbs, tubers, corms, and rhizomes. A bulb is simply an enlarged underground bud, such as that found with hyacinths, tulips, and onions. A tuber is an enlarged or modified root or stem; a common potato is a tuber; gloxinias, *Caladium*, dahlias, and many other common plants are grown from tubers. A corm is the enlarged base of a stem. And a rhizome is simply a laterally growing, enlarged stem, usually underground. All are used by the plant for food storage, and all can be used to propagate plants, too.

Water is constantly being drawn up through the plant. As it transpires through the stomata (pores) of the leaves, a pulling action draws more water up through the roots. The water carries with it mineral salts, including all the elements that the plant needs to carry out its complex chemical processes. The transpiration that takes place in the leaves is similar to perspiration in humans, and it serves a similar purpose—to cool the plant. With house plants this cooling effect is difficult to notice. But it is readily apparent when a group of large trees carry out the transpiration process. The cool and fresh feeling you enjoy in a thick woods in summer is not primarily the product of the shade itself but the transpiration of the millions of leaves overhead.

It is virtually impossible for a plant to absorb too much water, since its vessels and cells can accommodate only so much at a given time; however, the overwatering of a plant can exclude oxygen from the root system, ironically causing wilting of the top portion of the plant. When water is withheld, the plant's cells will gradually collapse, causing wilting of the entire plant. All plants do have protective mechanisms that conserve water in times of drought, though, and can withstand a temporary dry spell. Most wilted house plants will quickly spring back to a normal state when water is again provided.

PARTS OF A PLANT

Stem

The stem serves to support the plant and to contain and direct the vessels that transport water from the roots and food from the leaves to every other part of the plant. Most house plants, including *Philodendron*, ivy, and spider plant, have soft stems. Such plants must either climb or crawl, because their stems are not strong enough to support an upward-growing structure of significant height. Other plants have soft but thick stems that enable them to attain good height, although their stems are apt to be subject to breakage. Woody-stemmed plants, such as those of avocado, poinsettia, and boxwood, are far more sturdy and are usually derived from trees or shrubs of temperate regions. Canes are thick stems with hollow or pithy centers. Bamboo is an example of a cane with which we all are familiar; among house plants *Dieffenbachia* and ti plant are good examples.

Some plants have a distinct main stem, while others send up many stems, none dominant. A side shoot is a smaller stem growing out from the main stem. A petiole is a leaf stalk—the stemlike structure from which a leaf grows. A node is a joint on the main stem from which a leaf or side shoot grows.

Leaf

The major function of the leaf is, as we have seen, to manufacture food for the plant's growth and reproduction. Considering its total mass the leaf has a remarkably large surface area, ideally designed for the efficient absorption and diffusion of gases through its thousands of stomata.

After the basic functions of the leaf are understood, its proper care is not difficult to appreciate. The stomata must be kept fairly clean, free of dust and oil that might hinder their efficient operation. Leaves must also be given the freest access to light and ventilation, according to the individual preferences of each plant. Never crowd plants to a point where they are competing for light and air.

Roots

Roots serve two main functions—to anchor the plant in the ground and to supply, from the soil, water and the mineral salts that accompany water. Bulbs, corms, rhizomes, and tubers (all modified stems) serve much the same purposes, as well as acting as food storage areas. Roots, just as the aboveground parts of plants, may be pruned without injuring the plant in any way. Roots are often trimmed to prevent a plant from growing too large for the convenience of the grower, just as top growth is cut back. If you cut roots back, however, be certain to cut back top growth by about the same percentage, or the reduced roots might be unable to supply the plant with sufficient amounts of water. The major precaution in caring for roots is, as I will mention several times in these pages, to avoid overwatering.

Flowers

The plant's flowers contain its sexual apparatus. Pollination

occurs when pollen is deposited onto the stigmata, thus allowing the formation of seeds. The fruit of any plant is in reality
the mature or ripened ovary, which swells to protect the
seeds. In nature most plants produce flowers. For the purposes of cultivating house plants, only certain ones—which
in this book are listed as flowering house plants—can be
depended on to produce, under home conditions, blossoms
of sufficient size, profusion, and beauty to warrant our attention. The plants that we grow for their attractive foliage often
cannot produce flowers indoors because of insufficient light.
In nature pollen is most often transferred by insects or wind,
both of which are (we hope) lacking in the home. Where
indoor pollination is essential for seed or fruit production,
it can be accomplished by transferring the pollen from one
flower to another, using a soft camel's hair brush. This process is described fully in most books devoted to flowering
house plants.

SOIL AND POTTING MIXTURES

Since the house plant you bring home from the shop will
already be rooted in soil (presumably the shop knows its business), you might wonder why you have to consider this need
at all. The answer is that your house plant will, assuming
hoped-for longevity, someday need repotting, and you will
want to provide it with a potting mixture that will serve
its special needs. You might even wish to propagate some of
your favorite house plants to share with friends and to give
as gifts. In any case a basic knowledge of potting mixtures
and soils is essential to a complete understanding of all your
plants.

Two simple definitions are in order here to avoid any
confusion later. *Soil*, when mentioned here, refers to garden
loam, that combination of mineral matter, organic matter,
air, and water commonly found in your garden or under your
lawn. A *potting mixture* is soil with the addition of other
materials, such as sand, compost, peat moss, limestone, and

2 PARTS LOAM
1 PART COMPOST
1 PART BUILDER'S
   SAND
PINCH BONE MEAL
PINCH GROUND
   LIMESTONE

BASIC POTTING MIXTURE

bone meal, that together form an ideal environment for the roots of your house plants.

The easiest way to assure your plants of a perfect loam is to buy prepackaged, sterile potting soil from your garden center or flower shop. This soil will have not only the proper texture, but it will also be free of disease organisms, insects (some too small to be seen), and weed seeds. To this loam you will add the other ingredients, which together will form an ideal potting mixture. You may also buy packaged potting mixture—but if you do, read the package carefully to ascertain the ingredients, making sure that the mixture is right for your plants.

It is, of course, far less expensive to make your own potting mixture from your own garden loam (free), sand (free or next to free), and small amounts of purchased ingredients. If you choose this route, then it is important that you be able to make at least a cursory analysis of the garden loam that will form the basis of the potting mixture. Texture is important. A heavy clay soil will hold water for too long, encouraging disease and root rot, and it will bake cement-hard when dry. On the other hand, a coarse sand will not hold water well nor will it hold nutrients long enough for the plant's roots to absorb them. Strive, then, for a happy medium— a good loam, containing both clay and sand, that will hold both water and nutrients, yet offer adequate drainage. Be sure, also, to sterilize the soil by spreading it in a shallow pan and placing it in an oven (medium heat) for one hour.

To this basic loam we usually add one or more other materials—peat moss to increase water-holding capacity and to add organic matter, compost for organic matter and nutrients, sand to open the soil to air, and some form of supplemental mineral fertilizer, usually bone meal and lime. Chemical fertilizer can be used, although it is not necessary to add it to the potting mixture, since the other ingredients will supply all the nutrients the plant can use for several months.

ACIDITY/ALKALINITY

A discussion of soils and potting mixtures would not be complete without some mention of acidity and alkalinity and of the pH scale, which is the scientific measure for acidity and alkalinity. The midpoint on the pH scale is 7. A soil with a pH of 7 is neutral—neither acid nor alkaline. Numbers above 7 indicate an alkaline soil, those under 7, an acid soil. Most house plants, as most garden plants, will do best in a slightly acid soil (a pH of 6.0 to 6.9).

Most garden soils in the northeastern part of the United States are within this range, and gardeners there need not worry unduly about the pH of ordinary garden loam. In large areas of the southwestern states, however, the soil tends to be alkaline in nature, calling for the addition of agricultural sulfur. Your garden center manager can provide directions. In this book, all the plants listed will do well at a pH of 6.5 to 7.0, unless special notations to the contrary are made.

If you are concerned about your soil's pH or are simply curious, call your county agricultural agent and ask to have your soil analyzed for pH level. The cost will be nominal. Any soil may be made more acid with the addition of sulfur, or less acid with the addition of ground limestone.

POTTING MIXTURE RECIPES

There are as many different basic potting mixtures as there are plant experts—maybe more. Perhaps the most common one, however (and one that can be trusted), calls for two parts loam, one part finely screened compost (or a mixture of peat moss and compost), and one part builder's sand (not sea sand).* To this is added a small amount of bone meal (about one teaspoon for a five-inch pot) and a pinch of ground limestone. Other recommendations call for more of one ingredient and less of another. Do a little experimenting of your own. After a while you may find your favorite mixture, which you can recommend to others.

And now that you have the basic mixture formula well in mind, we will consider the exceptions:

1. Acid-loving plants, such as azaleas, camelias, gardenias, and heathers, should be given no lime. In fact, they should have some form of acid organic matter—acid peat moss or oak leafmold.

2. Foliage plants need somewhat more compost in the mixture, although half of it should be comprised of peat moss (which is low in nutrients and will not overstimulate the plant).

3. Fast-growing and hungry plants need more bone meal and lime, since they use them up quickly.

4. Some plants, such as cacti, succulents, and orchids, have very special soil requirements; these are mentioned later in the discussions of individual plants.

NUTRIENT MAINTENANCE

The mineral nutrients contained in any fresh potting soil or mixture, whether it is homemade or a sterilized commercial brand, should be sufficient for your plant's needs for the first four to six months. After that you should begin to replenish those nutrients on a regular and carefully measured basis.

All plants need substantial amounts of three elements—

---

*Throughout this book, builder's sand is recommended for potting purposes, while sea sand is cautioned against. Builder's sand, which comes from inland locations, has irregular and sharp surfaces, allowing good drainage. Sea sand, having been washed smooth over the years, packs too snugly and leads to a compacted soil and resultant drainage problems. Sea sand may also carry harmful salt deposits.

nitrogen (N), phosphate (P_2O_5), and potash (K_2O), and lesser amounts of a dozen or more others, called trace minerals or trace elements. In grower's language, the three major elements are referred to as N, P, and K, and on the label of any commercial fertilizer, the percentages of each are given in N-P-K order. A 5-10-5 fertilizer, for instance, will contain 5 per cent nitrogen, 10 per cent phosphate, and 5 per cent potash. A so-called "balanced" fertilizer contains a balance of all three in the amounts needed for the proper growth of most plants. The fertilizer may be either a chemical or an organic preparation, according to your preference. The chemical kinds are quick acting, easy to use, and tidy. Organic fertilizers, on the other hand, are slow to release their nutrients, providing a gentle and steady supply. Chemical mixtures come in liquid, tablet, and even spray form (the last applied directly on the foliage). Organic fertilizers may be purchased commercially in balanced formulas (fish emulsion, made from fish wastes, is a popular one for house plant use) or may be made at home from a combination of ingredients. Blood meal is a good choice for supplying substantial amounts of nitrogen (its NPK formula is 15.00-1.30-0.70), while bone meal (4.00-21.00-0.20) is good for phosphate and wood ashes (0.00-1.50-7.00) are high in potash content. A combination of one part blood meal, one part bone meal, and two parts wood ashes will make a 5–6–4 formula, which is a good one for house plants.

How often should plants be fertilized? The answer is unclear, because experts disagree sharply on the subject. But one thing is very clear: Do not fertilize as often, or as much, as recommended by the manufacturer of a commercial plant food. Manufacturers understandably overestimate the need for their products. The no-time gardener, furthermore, is looking not for wild and rank growth among house plants but for controlled growth and healthy plants. To achieve this goal go very easy on fertilizer of any kind. My personal policy is to apply half as much as the manufacturer recommends and only half as often, meaning that my plants get only one-fourth of the recommended feeding. Many more plants have been killed or injured by the overapplication of fertilizer than by mineral starvation.

If a plant shows a spurt of active growth in late winter or early spring, increase the dosage to the manufacturer's recommendation for a short while. During a dormant or rest period, withhold fertilizer entirely. If you are using a home-made organic fertilizer, such as the one suggested above, use it sparingly at first. A level teaspoon of the blood meal/bone meal/wood ash formula, applied monthly, should be plenty for a plant in a five-inch pot. You may also put some of the mixture in a bottle, fill the bottle with water, and use this "tea" to water your house plants. A mild tea solution, applied weekly, will give all your plants a continuing and gentle supply of the essential nutrients.

Last, remember never to apply a chemical fertilizer if the soil is dry. The quick action of the chemicals can easily injure the roots.

CONTAINERS

Nearly any container that offers adequate drainage and doesn't leak is suitable for house plants. After checking a container for leakage, consider drainage carefully. If the container has a hole in its bottom, there is no problem. If not, then you should put coarse gravel or broken crockery in the bottom of the container to fill one-fifth its depth. In this way you will avoid the likelihood of waterlogging your plants and encouraging root rot.

The traditional terra-cotta clay pot offers definite advantages. It is inexpensive, easily replaced, and—most important —allows air to be exchanged through its porous walls. This same porosity, however, allows water to evaporate fairly quickly, necessitating frequent watering. If a plant's location makes it awkward for you to water, you will save yourself some effort by choosing a glazed or otherwise impervious container.

Some metal containers, notably copper, might produce adverse chemical reactions with soil and fertilizer elements, injuring plants therein. Copper planters, however, are usually lacquered to prevent such reactions.

Wooden tubs and boxes are ideal for very large house plants. You can make any wooden container watertight by lining it with several sheets of heavy-gauge plastic or, for permanent results, sheet metal.

Finally, if you want the best advantages of both a terra-cotta pot and a decorative container, place the former inside the latter, leaving one-fourth inch or more of space for air circulation around the walls of the inner pot. Sometimes sphagnum moss is inserted here to help conserve moisture. A base of gravel in the decorative pot can provide good drainage while lifting the inner pot to the level of the outer container.

WATERING

More house plants are killed by overwatering than by any other cause. This killing with kindness can be avoided, if you learn to understand just when your plants need water and when they should be left alone.

The best rule of thumb is that a plant should be watered when the soil surface is dry to the touch. Then water thoroughly, either by adding water to the soil surface or by immersing the pot (up to but not over the lip) in a larger container of water.

With certain plants, such as African violets and other woodsy varieties, there are many conditions that call for more or less water, as indicated in Table 1.

Immersion is the best method of watering, because it is the surest. The soil in any pot might tend to form water channels, which, upon receiving water from the surface, will rush it to the bottom of the pot and out the drainage hole, leaving large parts of the soil bone-dry. Then some potting soil mixtures will shrink when drying, leaving many spaces along the wall of the pot where water can run past. Immersion is the one sure way to soak the soil thoroughly (provided that the pot is porous). You can do it in any large con-

tainer, a sink, or a bathtub. Set the potted plants in the water, but do not let the water flow over the lips of the pots. After the surface of the potting soil has become moist — ten to thirty minutes — remove the potted plant, drain off any excess water, and put it back in its place. Never go out for the afternoon, leaving your plants standing in water.

If you are thinking that the immersion method of watering takes more time that you are willing to spend in a no-work system, you might be right — except that you need not do it more than once every two weeks or so, to maintain plants in good health. Between immersions you can simply add water to the soil surface in the normal fashion. Even a monthly immersion will ensure that your plants do not develop harmful water channels.

When you water from the top, remember to remove any excess water from the saucer. Plants should never be allowed to stand in water for fear of root rot. In time, you should learn to give each plant just enough water to soak it thoroughly, with very little excess drainage. (And speaking of saucers, get glazed ones — not unglazed terra-cotta — if you want to protect your furniture.)

Some other watering tips:

1. Do not let water rest in the crown of any plant (the plant section at the soil surface), for this will encourage decay.

2. Never use very cold water, especially for tropical plants. Keep an open jar of water at room temperature for your house plants. Not only will the proper temperature be assured, but — if you use tap water — some of the chemicals will have dissipated by the time it is given to plants. This method takes no more time than others. It is simply a matter of filling the jars for the next watering *after* you have watered rather than before.

3. Water that is artificially softened may be detrimental to plant growth. There is also some evidence showing that fluorine is not good for some house plants. If you can, use rainwater or water that has not been softened.

4. If your water is especially hard, lime salts might cause trouble with such acid-loving plants as orchids, *Primula*,

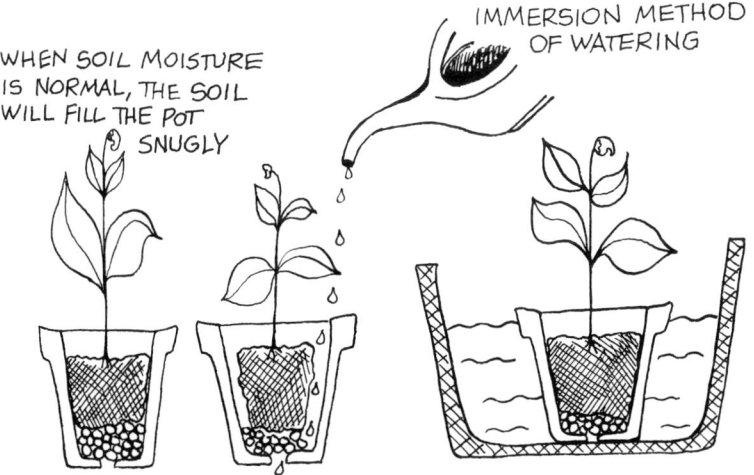

IMMERSION METHOD OF WATERING

WHEN SOIL MOISTURE IS NORMAL, THE SOIL WILL FILL THE POT SNUGLY

IF THE SOIL HAS DRIED OUT CONSIDERABLY, IT MAY HAVE SHRUNKEN, LEAVING WATER CHANNELS ALONG THE SIDES OF THE POT. WATER APPLIED FROM THE TOP MIGHT RUN THROUGH THESE CHANNELS QUICKLY, DEPRIVING THE SOIL AND THE PLANT OF NEEDED MOISTURE

THE IMMERSION METHOD IS BY FAR THE BEST AND SUREST WAY OF WATERING.

Rhododendron, azaleas, and others whose natural soil is woodsy (indicating a high organic content) and acid. Either choose plants that prefer a more neutral range in the pH scale, or plan to collect rainwater for your calcifuges (lime haters).

HUMIDITY

Much of our trouble with house plants, especially in winter in northern homes and in naturally dry areas of the country, can be traced to insufficient moisture in the air. Except for

Table 1. WATERING NEEDS OF PLANTS UNDER VARIOUS CONDITIONS

Plants will need more water when . . .	Plants will need less water when . . .
. . . they are in a period of active growth.	. . . they are in a period of rest (usually during winter).
. . . they are in bright light.	. . . they are in dim light or under artificial light.
. . . room humidity is low.	. . . room humidity is high.
. . . room temperature is high.	. . . room temperature is under 70°.
. . . they are contained in small pots.	. . . they are in large pots.
. . . they are in clay pots.	. . . they are in nonporous pots.
. . . they are fast-growing varieties.	. . . they are slow-growing varieties.
. . . they are planted in sandy soil.	. . . they are planted in heavy soil.
. . . they are in flower or about to go into flower.	

cacti and other succulents, nearly all house plants thrive best in a relative humidity of between 40 and 60 per cent, while that of most heated homes in winter is under 40 per cent — often considerably under 40 per cent. House plants will virtually cry for moisture under these conditions, and it is incumbent upon you to answer that cry.

There are several ways to add moisture to the air in your home. The more expensive include the adding of a humidifying device to your furnace, if you live in a house, or installing an electric humidifier. This step will benefit not only the plants but everyone living in the house, too. But there are less expensive ways to bring moist smiles to the faces of your plants:

The Pebble Tray

Line the bottom of a waterproof tray with decorative pebbles and arrange your plants, in pots, on top of the pebbles. Keep the tray filled with water, being sure only to avoid blocking the pots' drainage holes. Sprinkle a little charcoal among the pebbles to keep the water fresh. It takes no work to maintain the pebble tray, after it has been set up, since you simply keep the water level up as you water your plants.

Decorative Containers

If you keep a clay pot inside a decorative container (which is called double potting), keep a pool of water in the bottom of the larger vessel. Again, provide some means of support for the clay pot so that it is not resting in water at any time. Or fill the space between the walls of the two pots with wet sphagnum moss and keep it wet, in which case you will not have to maintain a pool of water.

Standing Water Devices

Water left standing in a room will gradually evaporate, meaning that the lost moisture is added to the room atmosphere. If your house or apartment is particularly dry during cold

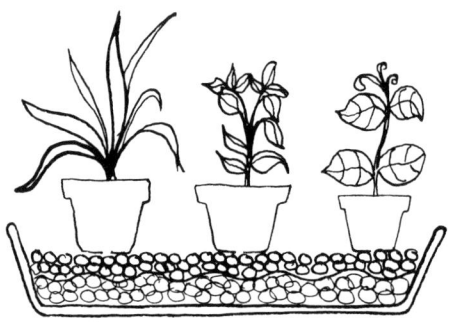

THE PEBBLE TRAY

ADD MOISTURE TO THE PLANTS'
IMMEDIATE ENVIRONMENT BY
KEEPING FRESH WATER IN THE
TRAY . . . BUT NOT TOUCHING
THE BOTTOMS OF THE POTS
OR BLOCKING THEIR
DRAINAGE HOLES

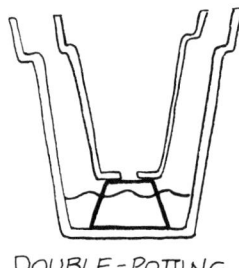

DOUBLE-POTTING
WITH STANDING
WATER

weather, take the trouble to place pans of water on tops of radiators or over heat vents; grow ivy, *Philodendron*, or wandering Jew in containers of water; maintain an aquarium; do anything, short of making a major project of it, to add water to the home atmosphere—even to the point of keeping a little water in the bathtub.

Bathroom Vacations

Rotate your plants occasionally so that each can spend an afternoon in the bathroom. If you are heading to the bathroom to take your morning shower, grab a house plant on your way, and let it soak up the humidity for the rest of the day.

(Remember that all the above suggestions can be implemented in odd moments during the day or evening. Special potting and setting up pebble trays will take some time, of course, but the regular maintenance takes only seconds, and can be done while you are waiting for dinner to cook or during a television commercial. The bit-and-snatch method makes the no-work method succeed!)

Plant Bathing and Showering

When the air is dry, most house plants will appreciate a brief misting every day or two or at least as often as you can manage to provide the treat. Little brass-plated atomizers are ubiquitous in mail-order catalogs and at house plant centers, but more dependable (albeit less decorative) are plastic sprayers available at house plant centers and art supply stores. These hold a pint or a quart of water and feature an adjustable shower head, affording an entire range of water action from a sharp jet capable of carrying twenty feet (the kids love this one) all the way to a fine mist. Your plants, of course, will like the fine mist. Remember to fill the container after every use, so that the following day's spray will be at room temperature. Remember also to avoid spraying plants that have been standing in direct sunlight (the shock is great) and those that have been subjected to very cool temperatures (perhaps spending the autumn on a cold sun porch).

Rubber plants and others with large leaves should be cleaned thoroughly and gently with a damp cloth every week or so. Commercially sold leaf polish is permissible, if you want really stunning looking, large-leafed plants, but never use any other kind of oil, since it can block the leaf's pores and impede respiration. Ivies and other rugged small-leafed plants can be held under the gentle stream of a faucet for their weekly bath.

Grouping

Plants will maintain moist surrounding air with greater facility if they are grouped together (leaves not touching) rather than separated. During the coldest part of winter, you might want to group most plants on a pebble tray under a light window to take advantage both of maximum light and greatest humidity.

VENTILATION

Plants, like people, benefit from fresh air. Like people, also, they react badly to drastic changes in air movement and temperature. Provide adequate ventilation for your house plants, but do not subject them to sharp winds, winter drafts, or heat rising directly from radiators or vents. Think of your own comfort in this respect, and you will know what will please your plants. If in autumn you bring your plants in from a summer outdoors, help them adjust to indoor conditions gradually by placing them by an open window for the first several days. Gradually lower the window day by day, keeping a watchful eye on night temperatures.

TEMPERATURE

The temperature requirements of house plants vary widely, according to the natural habitat of their forebears and also according to other conditions. Many cool-weather plants prefer a range of 50° to 60° and cannot tolerate temperatures above 70°, while tropicals may thrive in a moist 70° to 75°. Know the temperature preferences of any house plant before you adopt it, and then place it in the best possible temperature location in your home. You might find, for instance, that a cool-loving *Aspidistra* will do best in a back bedroom, while tropical plants thrive happily next to (but not above) a living room heat vent. A *Coleus* may perish where an African violet thrives and vice versa.

The temperature requirements or tolerances of plants are included in their descriptions throughout this book. Heed them well, make liberal use of an indoor thermometer, and do not be afraid to experiment by placing different plants in different locations for up to a month at a time. You might notice in your plants distinct preferences for particular locations throughout the house, and their preferences will not always corroborate expert advice.

AIR CONDITIONING

Some people have the mistaken idea that air conditioning is bad for plants. On the contrary, most house plants thrive in the constant, moderate temperatures that air conditioning provides. Cool-loving plants, in fact, may demand it for good health in the warmer sections of the country. The only caution is that no plant be placed directly in the path of a cold stream of air.

LIGHT

Light and temperature needs are closely related. In their native environments, many tropical plants can thrive at high temperatures, because they receive long hours of sunlight. In the home and especially during winter's short days, they cannot receive enough light to enable them to stand high indoor temperatures.

Except for most cacti and succulents, house plants should not be placed in windowsills where they will receive long periods of direct sunlight. Simply place a thermometer in this position; you will soon see that your plants can literally be cooked to death even in the dead of a Minnesota winter. Strive instead for a bright spot that receives filtered sunlight, at least for most plants.

Individual varieties differ in their light needs, of course, and these needs are specified in the descriptions of individual plants in these pages. Again, do not be afraid to experiment with different locations for different plants.

PREVENTIVE PRUNING

Most plants should be pruned and pinched back occasionally, in order to encourage bushy and stocky growth. Pinching back takes little time; it can be done in a few seconds simply by pinching off, between thumb and forefinger, much of the new growth of a plant. This pinching back, done in odd moments, will save much work, since you will never have to deal with rank and ungainly growth of any of your plants.

Many people hesitate to prune at all, feeling somehow that

PINCHING BACK OR STOPPING THE MAIN STEM WILL ENCOURAGE BUSHY SIDE GROWTH

MANY UPWARD-GROWING PLANTS, INCLUDING GERANIUMS AND FUCHSIA, WILL GROW TALL, LEGGY, AND WEAK WITHOUT REGULAR PRUNING.

WHEN PRUNING, ALWAYS TRY TO MAKE THE CUT IMMEDIATELY ABOVE A NODE OR BUD, WHERE NEW GROWTH WILL OCCUR.

they will hurt the plant or interfere with its natural development. Actually plants will respond to judicious pruning with new and bushier growth and vigorous health. Plants like geraniums, *Coleus,* and begonias should be pinched back routinely in order to encourage lateral growth. If you find that a plant is growing too tall, when you would prefer that it remain shorter and bushy, simply pinch back the growing tips at the top of the plant; or, if the growing tips are too thick, use a sharp knife. However you do it, the plant will respond by sending out side shoots below the central tip, and the main stem of the plant will then become thicker and sturdier. If this is done several times a year or even more often with quick-growing species, each plant should eventually attain the vigorous and well-rounded form you desire. Without any pruning or pinching back, a plant might grow "leggy" with a weak main stem, requiring some kind of support. Many older plants as well will benefit from occasional pinching back or shearing of outside growth.

There are a few house plants that should never be pruned or pinched back. They include Norfolk Island pines, African violets, gloxinias, flowering bulbs, succulents, ferns, and cyclamens.

In the no-work system of house plant raising, it is important that you take the little time required to prune and pinch back occasionally. Not only will you save much work in supporting leggy plants later on, but you will find that unchecked plants will also demand more water and fertilizer and more frequent repotting—all of which make more demands of your time.

If you want to reduce the time you spend in pruning and pinching back new growth, then reduce the plant's water supply (watering only when the surface is really dry) and cut back on fertilizer. Any plant can remain in good health with only two light applications of fertilizer each year.

PLANT SUPPORTS

Vines and trailing plants often need some kind of support,

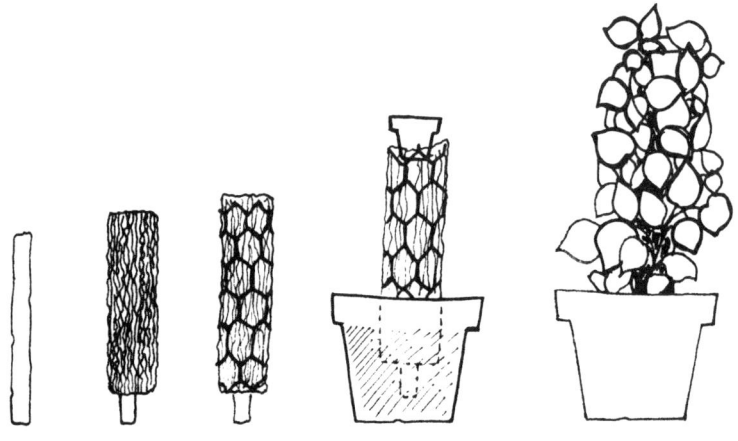

SPHAGNUM MOSS CYLINDER

unless you prune them severely or prefer to let them cascade from a hanging basket (which is usually preferred by no-work gardeners). Nevertheless, you may decide that the attractive appearance of a climbing plant warrants your time in giving it something to climb on. The usual practice is to sink a slab of cork or tree bark into a pot and then train the vines of the plant to grow around and up the support, eventually concealing it.

Another effective device is the sphagnum moss cylinder. Pack thoroughly wet moss fairly tightly around a stake and secure it in a cylinder of the proper diameter from the pot. The cylinder can be made easily from either wire mesh or green plastic material made for this purpose and available at house plant centers. If you wish, sink a small clay pot into the top of the cylinder, so that you can add water regularly to keep the moss damp. (Otherwise the moss will require regular spraying.) Tie the vines gently to the cylinder as they grow; eventually, *Philodendron*, ivy, and similar plants will anchor themselves to the moss, making other support unnecessary.

REPOTTING

If you don't overfeed plants or give them all the water they can possibly drink, you might never have to repot a plant. Nevertheless, at some time you might be seized with a peculiar gardener's malady that compels one to repot every plant in the house. If this ever happens to you, you must remind yourself that a plant needs repotting only when it has become pot-bound—when the roots have filled the entire container and are creeping from the drainage hole. If you find that a plant really needs repotting, then choose a new pot only one size larger than the old, for a house plant will not do well in a pot that is too large. If the larger pot has been used before, scrub it thoroughly to remove any possibility of disease. Soak new clay pots for a few hours until they become saturated. Then, with ample moist potting soil, gravel, and a tongue depressor or similar wood tool, set to work.

To remove the plant from its old pot, slide your hand over the top of the pot, index and second fingers cradling the plant stem. Turn the pot upside-down, thus supported, and tap the lip of the pot sharply on the edge of a bench or table. After a few taps the entire soil ball, ringed with plant roots, should come out easily, in one neat piece. Set it aside. Take the larger pot and line the bottom with a layer of coarse gravel or broken crockery to provide good drainage. Then add potting soil on top of the gravel, placing the plant and soil ball on top of the new soil several times to ensure that it reaches the proper depth. (The top of the soil should be about one-half inch below the lip of the new pot in a four-inch pot, and one inch below the lip in an eight-inch pot, to leave room for watering.) When enough soil has been added to raise the plant to its proper height, center it well; using the tongue depressor, begin to pack soil around the sides of the soil ball. Take your time in doing this, for it is the most crucial part of the entire operation. It is important

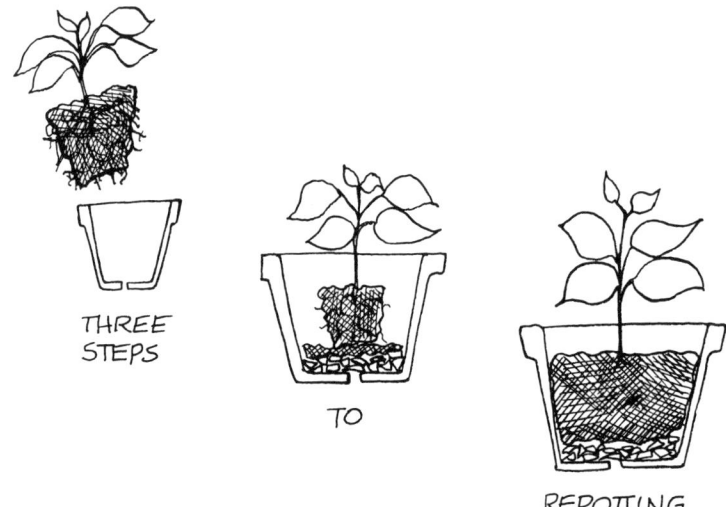

THREE
STEPS

TO

REPOTTING

to pack the soil firmly so that no air spaces are left. Roots cannot draw nutrients in air spaces, and many of them will thus be injured or die, affecting the health of the entire plant. When the new soil is finally brought to a level even with the top of the soil ball, the job is finished. You might want to add a little more soil over the top of the root ball, especially if roots have been forced up to the soil surface. But don't add any more than you must, for you do not want to change the planting depth of the plant. Repotting is shock enough for many plants without altering the planting depth. Water the plant thoroughly and return it to its usual location.

How often should you repot? Obviously, only as each plant indicates a need. For slow growers, this might be once every two or three years; a mature slow grower may go for many years without repotting, if new growth is cut back. For fast-growing and very young plants, repotting might be needed once or twice a year for the first several years. Plants that do not need repotting after one year should have the top one-half to one inch of soil replaced annually to keep their soil fresh.

40

PROPAGATION

A time may come when you want to start your own house plants—to increase your own plant population, to use as personal gifts for friends and family, or to replace a short-lived plant or one that has become ungainly with age. Propagation of most house plants is not difficult, and it is most rewarding.

There are two general methods of doing the job: by the collecting and planting of seeds and by the cutting and rooting of plant parts—stems, leaves, or underground structures. The first way (sexual reproduction) is usually less satisfactory than the second. Propagation from seed is ideal for garden annuals but not for most house plants. The seeds from hybrid plants are likely to produce plants vastly inferior to the parent plant. (A hybrid, incidentally, is any plant produced by cross-pollinating two plants of different varieties, species, or genera.) Last, many house plants do not flower and produce seeds under home conditions, requiring the house plant gardener to purchase seeds from specialty houses. The one advantage of growing house plants from seed is that you can create new hybrids by the cross-pollination of plants. The excitement of this activity creates a fascinating hobby for some house plant enthusiasts but is unlikely to appeal to those who cannot devote significant amounts of spare time to the activity.

Far more simple, and yielding far more reliable results, is the propagation of plants by the cutting and rooting of plant parts. Less care is required, and the offspring will look just like the parent, even when the parent is a hybrid.

Plants can be propagated at any time of year, though it is best to avoid tackling the job when the plant is going into a dormant period. Early spring, just before active growth begins, is perhaps the ideal time.

Cuttings

The most common method of propagating is by the taking of stem cuttings, which are then rooted in either water or some

41

sterile rooting medium such as perlite, vermiculite, or sand. If you have never rooted a cutting before, then begin with African violets, *Coleus*, *Dracaena*, *Fuchsia*, *Gardenia*, *Impatiens*, ivy, *Philodendron*, wandering Jew, or wax begonia. These are the easiest, because all can be rooted in water. Simply take a cutting, containing four to six leaves, from an actively growing tip of the plant, severing the stem cleanly just below a joint with a clean razor blade. Place the cutting (you may take several at a time from the same plant, if you wish) so that the bottom portion is submerged in water—a colored or clear bottle is fine—remembering only to keep the leaves above water. (Cut off the bottom leaf or two, if necessary, to get more of the stem into the water; about one-third of the entire length should be in water.) Place the container in diffused light—not direct sun—and wait until vigorous roots appear. When they have, the little plant may be removed from the water and potted in a small pot, using the potting mixture recommended earlier. Be sure to pack the potting mixture firmly around the roots of the plant to avoid any air spaces, and water thoroughly afterwards.

Stem cuttings that cannot be rooted in water are rooted in perlite, vermiculite (both available wherever house plant supplies are sold), or builder's sand. Be sure that at least one node is below the surface of the potting medium. The process is basically the same as for rooting in water. The cuttings are inserted in the moist medium, which may be contained in a small clay pot or, for larger numbers of cuttings, a shallow plastic tray. The planted container is then placed in a plastic bag, which is tied shut (the self-sealing kind, used for food storage, is convenient, effective, and reusable) and placed in diffused light at a temperature of 65° to 70°. You can tell whether the cuttings have developed roots by testing them weekly. Open the bag and pull gently on a plant. If it moves easily, then the roots have not yet formed; if it resists your gentle tug, however, then the roots probably are mature enough to stand repotting. The process can take as little as two weeks, or as long as several months, depending on the variety of the plant and the size of the cutting. When the roots are strong and vigorous, pot the plant in a small pot, and treat it as you would any other plant.

Some plants that produce canes (hollow or pithy stems), including Chinese evergreen, *Dracaena*, and *Dieffenbachia*, can be propagated by taking cuttings of the canes, which have discernible "eyes." Press each cane section (containing one eye) into moist sphagnum moss, secure it with wooden clothespins at each end so that it does not pop up, seal it in a plastic bag, and put it in a cool place out of direct sun. In six to eight weeks move it into a warm place (70° to 90°), still out of direct sun. Soon a shoot will grow from the eye. When the shoot has attained a respectable size, the cane may be cut close to the shoot on both sides, and the new plant may be lifted from the moss and potted.

Plants that have fleshy leaves are best propagated by taking leaf or leaf-petiole cuttings. (A petiole is a leaf stalk, or stem.) Leaf cuttings work well when large and mature leaves are available. Cut the leaf close to the stem of the parent plant, using a razor blade for a clean cut. The leaf may then be cut horizontally into smaller sections, so the main vein runs from top to bottom along the center of the leaf section. (Long-leafed plants like *Sansevieria* and *Streptocarpus* may be cut into as many as ten sections, each of which will produce an individual plant.) Each leaf section is then sunk halfway into the rooting medium, after which the process is the same as that described for stem cuttings. Patience is required here, for this method is often very slow to produce results.

Smaller leaves may be rooted by taking leaf-petiole cuttings. Cut one leaf stem close to the main stalk and sink the stem into the rooting medium; the leaf should almost (but not actually) touch the medium. African violets, begonias, snake plant, piggyback plant, and *Peperomia* respond well to leaf-petiole cuttings.

Underground Division

Older plants that have thick main roots can be propagated

by taking root cuttings. This is usually done when the plant is being repotted. Cut about one inch of the main root, making sure that it has at least one eye. Cover this with one-half inch of rooting medium, and treat it as you would any other cutting.

Thick-rooted perennials may be propagated simply by root division, in which the root mass is forced apart into two or more clumps, each of which is then repotted.

Plants that produce rhizomes may be propagated by dividing the rhizome so that one leaf bud is contained on each piece and planting the section under one-half inch of rooting medium. Plants that produce potatolike tubers can be propagated by cutting the tubers apart with a sharp knife, keeping one eye to each section, and planting the sections in the rooting medium just as you would plant potatoes in the open field.

Some plants produce "suckers," small plants that grow up from an underground stem or root. These may be separated from the parent plant and potted in soil immediately.

Anyone who has seen strawberries grow outdoors knows what runners are—the baby plants that grow from a long stem coming from the base of the parent plant. Among house plants, Boston fern, strawberry geranium, and spider plant produce runners, which can be started in a rooting medium and, only after they have rooted, severed from the parent plant.

Other methods of underground division include the separation and replanting of baby bulbs or corms, which are produced by the mother bulb or corm.

Air Layering

A fairly simple (and most impressive) way of propagating larger or woody-stemmed plants is by air layering. Here a sharp cut is made into the stem, perhaps a third of the way in, into which a toothpick is placed, horizontally, to keep the cut open. That stem section is then wrapped with moist sphagnum moss and covered with clear plastic and tied above

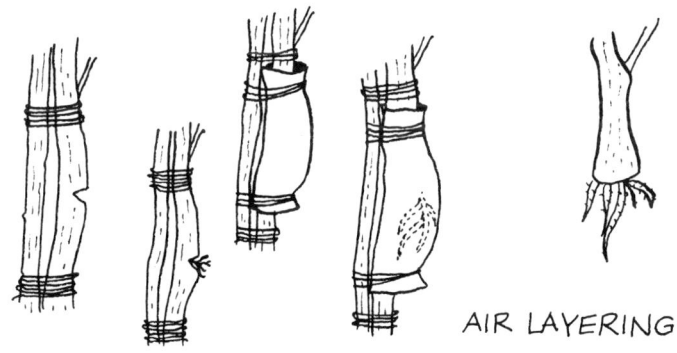

AIR LAYERING

and below so that moisture cannot escape. Roots will develop at the incision and will soon show through the plastic. When a fair number of them have appeared, cut the stem below the plastic wrap, remove both plastic and moss, and pot the new plant immediately in potting soil.

As you might imagine, the propagation of plants can often be integrated with the cutting back, pruning, and shaping of older plants. It seems a shame to throw away plant parts when they can be used to produce more plants. But precisely this attitude of thrift, if not controlled, can lead to a frightening multiplication of house plants. The answer, of course, is to share plants with friends, thus encouraging still more enthusiasts and still more house plants.

CAN YOUR PLANTS SURVIVE YOUR VACATION?

What will you do with your plants while you are gone for a long weekend, for a week, or for a month?

The best solution is to have someone come in to water them for you. Be sure to give the volunteer specific instructions, however, since anyone unfamiliar with the needs of house plants might easily kill them with kindness by overwatering them.

A long weekend should present no problem whatsoever,

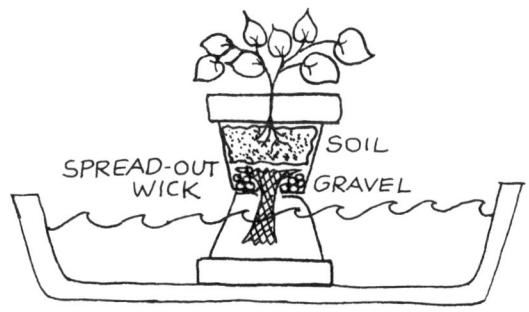

SPREAD-OUT WICK · SOIL · GRAVEL

except perhaps for vegetables and a few others that need daily watering. Simply soak your plants thoroughly by immersion and drain them; they should easily last for four days. If you will be gone for a week, enclose each pot in a plastic bag, and tie it snugly around the base of the plant stem. This device will cut surface evaporation greatly. Smaller plants can be enclosed completely in plastic bags, as long as some support is provided so that the plastic does not touch the foliage. Thus covered, most plants can remain in good health for at least a month. When uncovering them after your vacation, expose them to the outside air very gradually. They probably will have luxuriated in the greenhouse-like atmosphere of the plastic bag and can drop their leaves from shock if the bag is removed quickly.

Water wicks will keep a plant happy for weeks at a time. Wicks and pots are sold as units, usually called self-watering pots, but you can easily make your own at far less expense. Buy several yards of broad lamp wick. Cut off a six- to ten-inch section for each potted plant, depending on the pot size. Invert an empty pot in a larger container of water, until the water level comes to just below the top (the bottom, actually) of the inverted pot. Knock out the soil ball of the potted plant, insert the wick into the drainage hole, and flare out the end of the wick so that it covers as much of the bottom of the pot as possible (the wick should spread out above the drainage gravel just under the soil ball). Replace the soil ball

47

and plant. Thread the loose end of the wick through the drainage hole of the inverted bottom pot and into the water, and set the potted plant on the inverted pot. Water the plant once, from above, and the action should be continuous from then on. Test this method on several plants while you are still at home, in order to determine just how well it works for you and how long you can afford to be away from home without worry. It is a most effective method.

THE ABCs OF ARTIFICIAL LIGHT

The recent introduction of fluorescent light tubes meant especially for plant growing has been a great boon for the no-work indoor gardener. With the aid of these new lights you can now offer any plant the exact amount of intensity of light it needs for good health and controlled growth. With the addition of an automatic twenty-four-hour timer, you won't even have to remember to turn the light on and off. For your vacation periods and out-of-town trips, of course, the timer is ideal.

In addition, the new lights open up opportunities for you to expand your range of indoor gardening. Now you can grow lush, green plants in areas where they would never grow before. A windowless bathroom, which might offer ideal humidity and temperature conditions, can now be made into an ideal plant-growing environment. Plants growing on a drab northern windowsill can now receive supplemental light during winter's short, dark days. Dim corners of any room can be transformed into green showplaces. Under artificial light, cuttings and seedlings can now make faster and surer progress than ever, and we can even grow vegetables in the dead of winter in the bedroom or kitchen. Artificial lighting is not essential for house plant success, but it certainly does broaden our horizons, reduce work and worry, and increase chances for maximum rewards.

The old incandescent bulb does offer some help to growing plants, although the heat it produces makes it impossible to offer plants the amounts of light they need without drying or burning the plants. Also, incandescent bulbs offer a very short spectrum of light wavelengths, falling far short of simulating the beneficial rays of the sun. Ordinary daylight or cool white fluorescent lights are far better for growing plants, because they have not only a wider and more effective light wavelength, but they also produce light with three times as much efficiency as incandescent bulbs, thus reducing heat by fully two-thirds. Not until the past decade, however, have we had fluorescent tubes made to meet exactly the needs of growing plants. These lights, sold under such names as Gro-Lux, Plant-Gro, and Plant-Light, cost more than ordinary fluorescent tubes, but they are long lasting, and they can solve virtually any light problem for the indoor gardener. By attaching them to a twenty-four-hour timer you can control light exposure perfectly, even for such tricky operations as forcing plants to bloom out of season.

The best way to begin with artificial light is the most simple way. Purchase two forty-watt plant-growing tubes with the proper fixture, and hang it over a table where you will conduct your experiments. Be sure you have some method of raising and lowering the fixture, for you will want to adjust the lighting intensity to meet different plant requirements. Ferns and snake plants, for instance, have low light requirements, so the tubes should be placed twelve to eighteen inches above them; succulents, ivy, most flowering plants, and all vegetables have high light requirements, requiring the lowering of the tubes to eight inches or less above the plants. The closest you can bring the tubes and still avoid injury from heat is three inches above the plants. Guidebooks available from tube manufacturers give the exact light requirements of most common plants. In many cases excellent books on artificial light gardening can be found in your public library.

If you enjoy artificial light gardening and the gratifying results it brings, you will have no problem in expanding your activities in this area. Manufacturers have introduced a wide variety of special plant-growing stands, some with several tiers capable of holding dozens of plants, others decorative enough to enhance the beauty of any room. Your choices are

limited only by your imagination and your checkbook balance.

SHOULD YOU SEND YOUR PLANTS TO SUMMER CAMP?

In the northern states where the long winter has lulled most plants into a few months of rest and listlessness, nearly all house plants will enjoy a summer outdoors. In the South, however, gardeners will probably choose to bring plants into the air-conditioned comfort of the home or at least in the protective shade of the terrace or breezeway, when the summer sun reaches merciless intensity. Be guided by the needs and requirements of each plant, just as you are when they are indoors. Remember, too, that wind has a drying effect on all plants and that house plants outdoors must be watered more often than their indoor siblings.

Some dangers are involved in sending your plants outdoors at any time. Shock, resulting from either sharp light or temperature changes, is the main danger. Northern gardeners can avoid these by placing plants outdoors only when the night temperatures will go no lower than the minimum recommended for each plant. It might be best to put them on a sheltered porch or breezeway for the first few days, until they have become accustomed to the outdoors, or to put them out for only a few hours in the morning, bringing them in again before the heat of the day sets in. After a week or so they may be placed outside for the summer. Choose a spot shaded totally away from the sun. After a week of shade, those plants that can take some direct sun can be moved into diffused sunlight, perhaps under the protection of a large tree. Many house plants will be severely injured or killed by long exposure to a hot summer sun.

Keep the plants in their pots, and do not sink them directly into the ground because of soil insects and grubs. You may sink them, if you line the bottom of the hole with two inches of gravel, or they may be kept above ground, in which case you will have to watch soil moisture very carefully.

Check the plants every week for signs of insect infestation. If any appears, wash the plant thoroughly and bring it inside. Isolate it from other house plants, until all signs of the insects are gone.

Well before the first frost prepare to bring the plants indoors for winter. Again, inspect each for insect infestation. Wash each with a sharp spray of water. Knock out the soil ball, and inspect it carefully for insects or larva. Repot the plant at this time, if it is pot-bound. Prune back any excess growth that might have misshaped the plant; then bring it indoors. Keep it near an open, screened window for a week or two, in order to reintroduce it gradually to its indoor habitat, and then treat it normally. Your house plants should enjoy their summer at camp, even if they do act like sheltered children away from home for the first time. They should reward you with increased health and vigor that will last through the winter.

Southern gardeners often move their plants gradually onto porches, patios, and terraces as the temperatures begin to become moderate in autumn. As long as the outside temperatures are within the range required by the individual plant, the outdoor experience should be a refreshing and invigorating one. As winter approaches, the plants should be brought inside again or left outside for only the warmer hours of the afternoon. In early spring they can go outside again, when temperatures are favorable. The rule here is to avoid sharp contrasts in both temperature and humidity, either of which can injure the plant by sending it into shock.

The last word on this indoor–outdoor business is that you don't *have* to do it at all. In fact, the dedicated no-time gardener would flatly refuse (and quite correctly so) to run back and forth among house, porch, and backyard, carrying dozens of plants and checking weather forecasts at night. The house plants recommended in this book are perfectly capable of living in average home temperatures, even when they are on the high or low side of the permissible range. I offer the option, however, for those who might wish to give their plants optimum growth conditions for a few months of the year.

No-Work Foliage Plants

In this chapter we will survey many of the house plants grown primarily for their foliage. Some of them, under favorable conditions, will flower from time to time, although few should be selected for their flowering abilities. Nearly all of these plants are fairly easy to grow and maintain, giving the no-work gardener a wide variety of plants from which to choose.

The plants are listed in alphabetical order according to their common or popular names. If there is no popular name for a plant, or if there is more than one, none dominant, the plant is listed by its scientific or Latin name. The index, which includes both common and scientific names, provides a convenient means of cross-checking names.

The symbols next to each plant name will provide a quick and convenient guide to that plant's requirements. Remember, however, that these are guides and not sharp demands. Many of these plants are tolerant by nature and will take to an east window as well as an indicated west window; many can tolerate some direct sunlight even if none is recommended. Most crucial, perhaps, are the guides to humidity and moisture, since overwatering is one thing that few plants will tolerate.

On, then, to the foliage house plants:

AFRICAN BOXWOOD
(Myrsine africana)

This slow-growing plant has red stems but otherwise is similar to ordinary boxwood (see below). Many people think it is even more graceful. African boxwood is a good plant for terrariums, if the temperature there is not too hot.

ARALIA *(Fatsia japonica)*

Sometimes sold as *Aralia sieboldii*, this cheerful plant boasts beautiful, bright green, leathery, maplelike leaves. In appearance it is similar to the castor-oil plant and in fact is sometimes called false castor-oil plant. It thrives in a cool spot. Aralia can easily grow leggy, and so it should be pruned annually or even more often in order to encourage bushy growth. It will attain a height of four feet at maturity.

A striking hybrid, *Fatshedra lizei* (a cross between *F. japonica* and ivy or *Hedera*), forms a climbing plant with maple-shaped leaves; it is quite tolerant of adverse conditions. False aralia *(Dizygotheca elegantissima)* has graceful and feathery foliage. It bears no resemblance to the true aralia and is difficult to grow.

ARROWHEAD *(Nephthytis)*

This attractive plant is difficult to identify, since there is great confusion over what is and what is not a *Nephthytis*. Experts tell us that *Syngonium* is often mistaken for *Nephthytis*. Other experts say that most plants sold as *Nephthytis* are really *Syngonium*. Since the two plants are difficult to distinguish, however, no one cares very much except the experts. Whatever they are, they are tough plants, able to withstand adverse conditions. *Nephthytis* has large, arum-shaped leaves, compound at maturity but simple before that, and is either a trailer or a climber. Used as a climber it will have to have some support, such as that used by *Philodendron*. Propagation requires only the taking of stem cuttings.

Among several available species, the most popular is goosefoot plant *(Syngonium podophyllum)*.

ASPARAGUS

Two common kinds of *Asparagus* are suitable for growing as house plants: fern asparagus *(A. plumosus)*, with slender, needlelike, dark green leaves and a feathery appearance, and emerald feather *(A. sprengeri)*, which has thicker yellow green leaves and drooping stems. The latter makes a good plant for hanging baskets, and the older plants of this species produce red berries around Christmas. Both like some sun in the summer and full sun in the winter, and both can grow to a height of about two feet.

A. meyeri, less common but equally attractive, has tiny fernlike leaves that arch out on long stems from the center of the plant.

AUSTRALIAN LAUREL
(Pittosporum tobira)

Here is a tolerant and slow-growing plant whose glossy and leathery leaves resemble those of *Rhododendron*. Australian laurel will grow vigorously bushy and does not ask much attention. Florists often use the leaves in floral arrangements.

An interesting variegated form is *P. tobira variegata*, which grows quite large.

AUSTRALIAN UMBRELLA TREE
(Schefflera actinophylla)

This very attractive and vigorous-growing treelike plant has rich and glossy leaves that radiate umbrellalike from the ends of several leaf stalks. It is a tough and rewarding plant, growing to six feet, which can be propagated by air layering.

Australian umbrella tree is also sold as *Brassaia actino-phylla*. A dwarf variety, *B. actinophylla compacta*, is also available.

BABY'S TEARS *(Helxine soleirolii)*

This low creeper is also called Irish moss. It likes a constantly moist (but not soggy) soil and higher than average humidity. It makes a good ground cover for terrariums but will also grow in a pot if adequate humidity is provided. Baby's tears may appear to die in colder months, but after an adequate rest period it will spring back to life. It is very sensitive to fertilizer burn and salt accumulation.

BLACK PEPPER *(Piper nigrum)*

This is not an especially attractive house plant, but it produces real peppercorns that you may use at the table and is a good conversation piece for that reason. The plant's green berries eventually turn red, then dry up and turn black. Pick the dried black corns, dry them thoroughly for several weeks in an open spot, and then use them in your pepper grinder. The care for black pepper is the same as that required for *Philodendron* (see below). It is not a demanding plant.

Note: Be sure that you have this plant and not one of the so-called black peppers of the deadly nightshade family!

BOXWOOD *(Buxus)*

The same plant that grows the most prized hedges outdoors can make a very attractive house plant. Boxwood, with its glossy, bright green leaves, is slow growing and dependable, a good subject for bonsai, the ancient oriental art of growing dwarf trees and shrubs. Japanese boxwood *(B. microphylla japonica* and *B. sempervirens)* are the two most popular species.

BROMELIADS

There are more than eighteen hundred varieties of this popular group, many of which are suitable for growing as house plants. Some of them produce attractive flowers, but most are grown for their striking and variegated leaf patterns. One distinctive feature of a bromeliad is the rosette of leaves that forms a small water cup, which the plant uses to hold reserve supplies of water in its natural habitat. Since the plant lives in the crotches of trees in Central and South America, the water cup is an evolutionary survival characteristic. In the home keep the cup filled with water, changing it weekly to keep it fresh.

Common bromeliads include *Aechmea*, pineapple *(Ananas)*, *Billbergia*, *Cryptanthus*, *Dyckia*, Spanish moss *(Tillandsia)*, and *Vriesia*.

CALADIUM

Caladium, with its spectacularly colored and variegated leaves, is equally at home in the outdoor garden and on the windowsill. It is an ideal addition to plant groupings on porch or patio in the summer and early autumn. Give it bright light but not long periods of direct sun in summer, if you want the brightest leaf colors. It will not last more than a season and should be treated as an annual.

Caladium is grown from a tuber, which can be divided easily to produce new plants. Start the tubers in regular potting soil at a very warm temperature—80° to 90°—and move the young plant to a cooler spot when it has appeared. It will attain a height of about one foot.

CAST-IRON PLANT
(Aspidistra eliator)

This is perhaps the easiest plant in the world to grow, as its name suggests. It is virtually impossible to neglect it to death. It is also called saloon plant, since it was one of the

57

few that could survive in Victorian taverns. And it was made immortal by George Orwell in his novel *Keep the Aspidistra Flying*. If you cannot grow *Aspidistra*, you may safely conclude that you have a hopeless case of purple thumb and had best invest in plastic plants.

Cast-iron plant, which grows about two feet tall, seems to thrive even better when kept slightly pot-bound, and it will appreciate having its leaves washed occasionally. An attractive white-striped species is *A. variegata*.

CHAMAERANTHEMUM IGNEUM

This low, spreading herb has attractive dark green leaves with reddish yellow veins. It is suitable for hanging baskets or as a low contrast in large plant groupings. It does like warm temperatures and high humidity, however, and might not do well in dry rooms.

CHINESE EVERGREEN *(Aglaonema)*

Here is an attractive plant that is very easy to grow. It will stand abuse nearly as well as the cast iron plant.

There are at least ten common species of *Aglaonema*, the most popular of which, *A. modestum*, has interestingly mottled leaves. Perhaps the prettiest, however, is *A. pseudobracteatum*, which is often difficult to find in shops and garden centers.

CISSUS

Cissus is a viny genus that offers a number of interesting and attractive species. Most are vigorous climbers, suitable for training on a trellis or for adding to hanging baskets.

Among the more popular species are grape ivy *(C. rhombifolia)*, which is one of the most popular and easy to grow of all house plants; kangaroo vine *(C. antarctica)*, which prefers a small pot; miniature kangaroo vine *(C. antarctica minima)*;

C. rotundifolia; and begonia ivy *(C. discolor),* which is perhaps the most spectacular of the genus, although it is difficult to grow.

COLEUS

This old favorite has leaves (some velvety) sporting bright splashes of reds, pinks, purples, and yellows. There is a seemingly endless number of varieties of *Coleus,* nearly all of them interesting, most growing twelve to eighteen inches in height.

Coleus is equally happy outdoors, grown as an annual in the North, or in the window garden. It can be grown easily from seed, and stem tip cuttings can be taken from established indoor plants nearly any time of the year. If you grow *Coleus* outdoors in summer, take some cuttings before the first autumn freeze, and root them for growing as house plants.

The soil for *Coleus* should be kept damp but not soggy. Pinch back plants often to encourage bushy growth.

COPPER LEAF *(Acalypha wilkesiana)*

These are members of the spurge family, which features copper-colored foliage. A close relative, chenille plant *(A. hispida),* is described below under the section on flowering plants.

Copper leaf may be propagated easily by taking cuttings late in the summer. The plant is susceptible to attack by spider mites, and proper precautions should be taken against this menace.

DICHORISANDRA REGINAE

This is a handsome, slow-growing plant with interesting leaf markings. It resembles wandering Jew but grows upright.

Give it warm temperatures and not too much direct light, but do watch room humidity.

DIEFFENBACHIA

There are many species of this popular plant, often called dumbcane. It is prized for its large leaves with interesting markings, usually variations of cream and white on dark green. *Dieffenbachia* is a fairly tough plant and is not too difficult to grow. Most varieties attain a height of eighteen to twenty-four inches, although growth is slow.

D. arvida 'Exotica' is very popular, because it is even more durable than other members of the family. Other well-known species include *D. picta*, *D. amoena*, *D. sequina*, and *D. bowmannii*.

There are no special cultural requirements, although *Dieffenbachia* does like a warm spot and will appreciate having its foliage cleaned regularly. The plant may be propagated by taking stem cuttings and rooting them in moist and warm peat.

Caution: Eating or nibbling on the leaves of *Dieffenbachia* can cause severe swelling of the tongue and mouth tissues, hence its popular name, dumbcane. It is *not* a plant to grow in a home with toddlers.

DRACAENA

The many species of *Dracaena* vary so greatly in appearance that some appear to be unrelated. Most grow tall—five feet or more—on sturdy stalks. They are very tough plants, tolerant of a surprising amount of neglect. All in all they are one of our most dependable house plants.

Some varieties to investigate are *D. deremensis* 'Warnecki,' *D. fragrans* (which has cornlike leaves), *D. fragrans massangeana* (whose leaves feature yellow stripes), *D. marginata* (a truly exciting plant, with grasslike, cream-colored foliage, edged in red—sometimes sold as *D. marginata tricolor*), *D.*

sanderiana (with white-banded leaves), *D. godseffiana* 'Florida Beauty,' *D. draco* (the dragon tree of the Canary Islands), and many others, some of which will doubtless be offered by any good supplier. These mentioned, however, are some of the most attractive and also some of the easiest to grow.

EPISCIA

This genus, which offers many species and subspecies, is related to the African violet and requires largely the same culture, although it does demand a little more light. *Episcia* is not really one of the easiest plants to grow successfully and should be tried only after success has been attained with some of the others listed here. The leaves are a rich green; most varieties are tinged with copper, some with variations of silver, blue, purple, and bronze. The veins often offer striking color contrasts. *Episcia* is a trailing plant, a natural selection for hanging baskets. It also sends out runners that may be used for propagation.

Most species of *Episcia* produce small, delicate flowers, in the color range of red-orange-yellow, but the plant is generally grown for its delightful foliage. If you do not wish to strive for blossoms, a north window will suit *Episcia* well enough.

The most popular species is *E. cupreata* (flame violet), which has soft, hairy, copper-tinged leaves and comes in several attractive varieties. Also investigate *E. dianthiflora*, which produces white flowers, and *E. lilacina* 'Cuprea,' with lavender flowers. Many other species and subspecies are easily available, all of which have fascinating foliage variations and some of which will bloom quite profusely.

FATSHEDRA
See Aralia.

FATSIA JAPONICA
See Aralia.

61

FERNS

Ferns are the oldest plants—on the evolutionary scale—that you are likely to cultivate. They are predated only by algae and mosses. Everyone knows and admires ferns for their graceful, feathery fronds. They are among the few house plants that reproduce themselves by spores rather than by seeds. Some ferns grow regally upright, while others trail with modesty and grace. There are many sizes of ferns, from miniature plants suitable for the windowsill all the way to the seven-foot tub plants that can add a touch of class to entryways, patios, and conservatories.

The secret to the successful raising of ferns is in offering them an environment matching, as nearly as possible, that of their natural habitat. They need warmth, a decent degree of room humidity (not under 30 per cent), and a moist and humusy soil (at least 50 per cent organic matter). They appreciate bright light but will be affected adversely if allowed to stand for long periods of time in direct sun.

There are a great many ferns from which to choose. Among the smaller ones are these:

The maidenhair fern *(Adiantum)*, is available in several varieties. It sends forth fragile-looking fronds in sprays and needs good light and high humidity. It is a rather difficult plant, probably not suitable for the real no-time gardener.

Asparagus fern *(Asparagus plumosus)*, the most popular of the small "ferns," is really not a fern at all but a member of the lily family and reproduces by seeds rather than spores. It is treasured for its delicate, hairlike leaves.

Other smaller "ferns" of the *Asparagus* group include simlax *(A. medeoloides)*, a trailer; emerald feather *(A. sprengeri)*, a climber; break fern *(Pteris multifida)*; chain fern *(Woodwardia orientalis)*, hare's-foot fern *(Polypodium aureum)*; and many others of a similar nature.

Among the larger true ferns are these:

Holly fern *(Cyrtomium falcatum)* has holly-shaped fronds. Bird's-nest fern *(Asplenium nidus)* has broad lance-shaped fronds. *Nephrolepis exaltata* has long, sword-shaped fronds and is often called sword fern. *N. exaltata* 'Bostoniensis,' is the ever-popular Boston fern. Staghorn fern *(Platycerium bifurcatum)* has fronds which are usually attached to a piece of bark or other support. They can become parched quite easily in a dry atmosphere.

The world of ferns is a large one, full of interest, and extremely rewarding. No house plant collection should be without at least one or two representatives of these proud families. If you have never grown ferns before, start out with the asparagus fern or the break fern, which are probably the easiest to grow.

FICUS

This large group of indoor plants, whose best-known member is the rubber plant, offers species ranging from large, treelike plants to small-leafed trailers. Although they are not difficult plants to grow, the large species are especially sensitive to both overwatering and sudden temperature changes and will react to either by dropping their leaves. For this reason, the no-time house plant grower might prefer to skip them entirely.

There has been much improvement in the rubber plant *(F. elastica)* since World War II. The best now is perhaps *F. elastica* 'Robusta,' which is remarkably trouble free. There are many decorative varieties, as well, including *F. elastica* 'Doescheri,' which has light and dark green patched leaves and cream-colored leaf margins, and *F. elastica* 'Schryveriana,' another mottled-leafed variety. *F. elastica* 'Decora,' from which 'Robusta' was developed, is still a popular slow-growing variety that will appeal especially to no-time indoor gardeners. Most rubber plants will grow as tall as any room but may be cut back to encourage bushiness.

Chinese banyan *(F. retusa)*, another treelike *Ficus*, showers forth a profusion of small, leathery leaves. Indian laurel *(F. retusa nitida)* resembles mountain laurel.

The fiddleleaf fig *(F. lyrata)* is a tough and attractive tree-like species with large, dark green, fiddle-shaped leaves. It needs warmer conditions than other *Ficus.* Weeping fig *(F. benjamina)* is another *Ficus* tree that has small, densely growing foliage; it is especially sensitive to low humidity and is likely to be worrisome. Mistletoe fig *(F. diversifolia)* is an easy-to-grow species that features yellowish berries in profusion.

The genus also contains many small plants. Most popular perhaps is creeping fig *(F. pumila),* a small-leafed creeper that has been developed to include several variations—*F. pumila minima,* slower growing and smaller, and *F. pumila variegata,* a variegated variety. All will adhere to rough surfaces, sending out aerial roots similar to those of ivy, and all are easily trained.

The tree-type *Ficus* are propagated by air layering, while the small-leafed climbers and trailers may be reproduced easily by simple division or cuttings.

GERMAN IVY *(Senecio mikanioides)*

This plant is similar to the true ivies in both appearance and requirements (see Ivy). A handsome relative is cape ivy *(S. macroglossus variegatus).* For easy success treat them in every way that you would treat ivy.

GINGER *(Zingiber officinale)*

This is the same ginger that is used in cooking, which makes the plant even more interesting than its appearance would indicate. The untreated rhizomes sold in specialty food and gourmet shops can be planted directly in potting soil to produce plants, or established plants may be divided easily. The plants have reedlike stems and exotic-looking grassy foliage. Success as a house plant depends on giving ginger plenty of sunlight and warm temperatures. Keep the soil constantly damp but never soggy for long periods of time. As an added bonus, healthy plants will bear colorful clusters of flowers. A rest period is required for this plant.

GOLD-DUST PLANT *(Aucuba japonica)*

This modest plant features dark green leaves spotted with yellow gold markings. Its main attribute is that it will withstand very cool temperatures, all the way down to freezing, and still come up smiling. It is good for unheated winter porches in all but the coldest parts of the country. Two popular varieties are *A. japonica variegata* and *A. japonica goldeana.*

GOOSEFOOT PLANT
See Arrowhead.

IVY *(Hedera)*

Ivy is surely one of the most popular of house plant species, both easy to grow and cheerful and attractive in appearance. The great number of varieties is continually enhanced with new improvements.

English ivy *(Hedera helix)* is the most popular of the true ivies and is available in more than fifty varieties to suit nearly any taste. There are varieties with large leaves and small, fast or slow growing habits, plain green or variegated colors. The best way to choose an English ivy to your liking is to visit flower shops and greenhouses or to beg a few cuttings from a friend who has a plant that appeals to you.

Propagation of ivy is easy, and in fact the plant does half of the job for you. Small rootlets will form on the stem of the plant, just below the leaves, which the ivy uses to attach itself to rough surfaces, helping it to climb. Make cuttings just below the rootlets, and plant these cuttings directly in potting soil or a sterile rooting medium.

It would be fruitless to attempt to recommend all the good varieties of English ivy. For a starter, however, you might investigate Japanese ivy *(H. helix conglomerata)*, an upright-growing plant with small, densely growing leaves; 'Curlilocks' and 'Ivalace' with curled leaf margins; 'Green Ripples,' 'Maple Queen,' 'Merion Beauty,' 'Needlepoint,' 'Pittsburgh,' 'Pixie,' 'Rochester,' *H. helix scutifolia*, and 'Shamrock,' the last of which likes more than average moisture and which is good for terrariums.

Among the variegated English ivies, try 'Golddust,' 'Glacier,' and 'Goldheart,' the last of which has dark green leaves with sharply contrasting bright yellow centers.

Canary Islands ivy *(Hedera canariensis)* is another easy-to-grow ivy, which has larger leaves than English ivy. It is often trained around a piece of bark, much like a *Philodendron*, to form a striking plant with a very bushy appearance. The no-time gardener, however, will probably prefer to let it trail from a hanging basket. More popular than the basic green-leafed variety is the variant *H. canariensis variegata*, also known as 'Glorie de Marengo,' whose leaves are slate green to cream in color.

JOSEPH'S COAT *(Alternanthera)*

These are low-growing, dwarf plants that are good for terrariums. Their multicolored foliage adds brightness to any plant grouping. Joseph's coat needs warm temperatures and a moist soil to be happy.

Note: *Codiaeum* is also called Joseph's coat, but it is a much larger-growing plant. Don't confuse the two.

MARANTA

Here is a genus of plants that has striking foliage. It is not very difficult to grow and will reach a height of about eight inches.

Prayer plant *(M. leuconeura kerchoveana)* is perhaps the most popular *Maranta* and is so named because its leaves fold up at night, as if in prayer. The leaves are large and oval, and the plant requires a fairly humid atmosphere. In the autumn some leaves may begin to die. If so, do not be alarmed. Cut off the affected leaves, and reduce watering until late winter, when new growth begins; then water normally.

A red-veined variety, even more striking, is *M. erythroneura*. Another with red veins is jungle plant *(M. leuconeura erythrophylla)*, which has olive green leaves. Still another handsome variation is offered by *M. leuconeura massangeana*.

Most house plant growers will want to include at least one *Maranta* among their collections. The key to success with this plant is in giving it lots of bright light but no direct sun at all.

MINIATURE HOLLY
(Malpighia coccigera)

This is not a true holly but is a bushy evergreen shrub with dense hollylike foliage. The leaves are shiny and dark green, and have spiny teeth. Miniature holly does produce small flowers, but it is grown primarily as a foliage plant. It is propagated easily from cuttings.

NORFOLK ISLAND PINE
(Araucaria excelsa)

This popular evergreen, graceful and symmetrical, is seen with increasing frequency. It will hold up well under adverse conditions, although its branches will droop in dim light. Give it a damp (but not soggy) soil, for it is very susceptible to overwatering. It does well when kept slightly pot-bound.

Norfolk Island pine is a slow grower and should never be pruned. It will grow gracefully to a height of about six feet, after which it tends to become ungainly.

PALMS

Here is a plant family full of nostalgia for many of us. In Victorian times and through the 1930's and 1940's, the potted palm was a symbol of exotic elegance, bringing a bit of the tropics to shivering northerners. The elegant palms lost much of their allure after World War II, but now they are making an impressive comeback.

You can achieve success with palms by giving them bright light (even though they will endure shade), relatively little water, and no plant food during winter. Palms actually seem to thrive on inattention, doing well when slightly pot-bound. They are slow growing in any case.

The palms are a plant family—*Palmae* is the scientific name—that comprises many genera and far more species. Few, however, are both attractive and manageable as house plants. Here are some palms you might wish to investigate:

European fan palm *(Chamaerops)* has fan-shaped leaves on long stalks and will become quite large at maturity.

A coconut palm species *(Cocos)* is at its best in the dwarf species *C. weddelliana*.

The familiar palm court palm *(Howeia)* is among the most popular of all indoor large palms. *H. belmoreana*, thought by many to be the most stunning species, can eventually grow to ten feet or more in height, given many years and sufficient room.

Neanthe is an agreeable and easy-to-grow dwarf that can tolerate a dry room.

The date palm *(Phoenix)* can be grown easily from the stone of a fresh date. Plant the stone in potting soil, and keep it warm (70° to 80°); it should germinate in about a month. It is slow growing during the first year or so, but within ten or fifteen years it will become as tall as any room.

PELLIONIA

This colorful, slow-growing, creeping plant is fine for hanging baskets and is a good filler plant for groupings. It has small, oval leaves with interesting variegated patterns. Two popular varieties are *P. daveauana* and the more compact *P. pulchra.*

Pellionia is not difficult to propagate. As it creeps along the soil, it sends down roots from the stems. Just cut the stems into sections, and root them in potting soil.

PEPEROMIA

There are many species and varieties of this popular and cheerful little plant (eight inches or less in height), most of which are low and upward growing, some with deeply ridged leaves. They are tough plants, tolerant of most conditions, although they will rot at the groundline, if the top of the soil is not allowed to dry out between waterings. *Peperomia* like bright light but not much direct sun in the summer.

Among the more popular varieties are the following:

Emerald ripple peperomia *(P. caperata)* has deeply ridged heart-shaped leaves; the tops of the ridges are green and the valleys are brown, giving an appealing effect.

P. rotundifolia is a low grower with light green, thick leaves.

Oval-leaf peperomia *(P. obtusifolia)* has solid green leaves, while *P. obtusifolia variegata* is the variegated form of the same species.

Watermelon peperomia *(P. sandersii)* is identified by its red petioles and silver-striped leaves.

P. grieseo-argentea hederaefolia has ridged, glossy, silver-hued leaves and purple olive veins.

There are many other varieties of the *Peperomia*, some of which may be seen at your local flower shop or greenhouse.

PHILODENDRON

These plants constitute what is probably the most popular

group of house plants in America today. There are many, many species and varieties, with leaves ranging from small to very large, in an assortment of shapes offered by no other house plants. Most are climbers and will appreciate a support that can be kept moist, such as that described on page 38.

Philodendron are not difficult plants to grow, unless you disregard the rules. Growth will be stunted by poor light, and the leaves can turn yellow and drop from lack of water, too small a pot, low temperatures, or poor drainage. They will appreciate a monthly washing with a mild soap (not detergent) solution. Cut back the growing tips if you wish to encourage bushy growth, and use the tip cuttings to form new plants.

You may wish to try one of these popular varieties:

Sweetheart vine *(P. scandens)* is a very popular climber that can withstand the dry air of a typical apartment. *P. oxycardium*, the most commonly grown form, has heart-shaped leaves very similar to *P. scandens*. It is often grown in water or wet moss. Cut-leaf philodendron *(P. dubium)* is a slow grower with star-shaped leaves. Fiddleleaf philodendron *(P. panduraeforme)* has irregularly shaped, olive green leaves. *P. pertusum* has irregularly shaped perforated leaves. The adult form, known as *Monstera deliciosa*, has broad, thick leaves with many perforations.

Anchorleaf philodendron *(P. squamiferum)* has leaves and petioles that are covered with red hairs. The leaves are shaped like daggers. Twice-cut philodendron *(P. bipinnatifidum)* is a large-leafed variety; the leaves resemble the smaller *P. dubium* in shape but are more deeply notched. *P. selloum* is another cut-leaf variety, with the cuts becoming more pronounced as the plant reaches maturity. This species will tolerate temperatures down to freezing with no apparent harm. *P. wendlandii* is another large-leafed species and is very tolerant of a wide range of temperature and humidity. Its leaves are long and narrow.

PIGGYBACK PLANT
(Tolmiea menziesii)

A native of the West Coast of the United States, this modest-sized plant can be grown outdoors in the warmer regions of the country. Its name is derived from its unusual habit of bearing young plantlets from the junction of the leaf and the petiole. These can be rooted easily to grow new plants. The leaves are toothed, lobed, and covered in down. It is an easy plant to grow.

PILEA

There are at least four cultivated house plants in this interesting group, none of which grows more than a foot in height. All like moist soil, warm temperatures, and full sun in the winter. The plants become less attractive as they grow older, but cuttings are easily made so that older plants may be discarded when desired. Fertilize *Pilea* liberally when growth is active.

Aluminum plant *(P. cadierei)* has dark green leaves with striking aluminum-colored markings. A dwarf variety, *P. cadierei minima*, is preferred by many, as *P. cadierei nana*, a compact variety. Artillery plant *(P. microphylla)* is fine in texture with bright green, fernlike leaves. When its flowers are dry, pollen literally explodes from the blossoms, hence its common name.

South American friendship plant *(P. involucrata)* is bushy in growth and has coppery leaves. It can be made to be even more bushy, if several cuttings are taken and then rooted in the same pot, to the sides of the parent plant. *P.* 'Silver Tree' has bronze-hued leaves with silver markings.

PLECTRANTHUS

Various species of this genus are often called trailing coleus

71

or Swedish ivy. Some are upright in growth, while others are trailers, making good subjects for hanging baskets.

P. australis, a trailer, has waxy green leaves, round in shape with sawtooth edges. *P. australis variegatus* is similar in leaf shape and has added white markings. *P. purpuratus* is an upright growing plant with purple coloring on the undersides of its leaves.

There are other interesting varieties, including *P. oertendahlii*, a flowering trailer with bronze-hued leaves and silvery veins.

PLEOMELE

This is an interesting group of plants with cultural requirements similar to those of *Philodendron*.

Song of India *(P. reflexa variegata)* is included by some in the genus *Dracaena*. Its attractive, spear-shaped leaves are gold and green striped, borne in clusters on branching stems. It will grow to tree size in ten or fifteen years.

P. reflexa gracilis has dense foliage; its recurved leaves have translucent edges. *P. thalioides* has waxy green leaves, ribbed lengthwise.

POTHOS *(Scindapsus)*

Pothos is very similar in appearance and growth habits to the heartleaf *Philodendron scandens*, but it needs less water and warmer temperatures—not below 65°. It likes bright light but cannot stand direct sun. Pothos is a natural trailer, although it can be trained upward along a support, again like *Philodendron*. The leaves are heart-shaped and green with pale yellow markings.

The most popular species is *S. aureus*, which offers several variegated varieties, some of which require even warmer temperatures.

RUELLIA MAKOYANA

This is an old favorite, not seen as often today as in the 1930's. It is a free-spreading plant, with glossy, pale green leaves with silvery veins. It likes a warm, moist environment, shaded from the sun.

SANCHEZIA NOBILIS GLAUCOPHYLLA

This member of the *Aphelandra* group grows to a height of four feet. It has large, glossy, sword-shaped leaves with yellow veins.

SCREW PINE *(Pandanus)*

This old favorite will withstand most adverse conditions. It is recognized by its long, arching swordlike leaves, which have sawtoothed edges.

P. veitchii has green and white striped leaves. Often preferred, however, is *P. veitchii compactus*, a dwarf variety with clearly variegated leaves. *P. baptistii* has no marginal spines, as do the other species. All screw pines like moist soil but never soggy soil. They can take some direct sun except in the heat of summer, although they do best in a bright location out of direct sun altogether.

SELAGINELLA

Among these fernlike plants are some small creepers, some erect-growing species, and some trailers. All offer bright green, feathery foliage. The conditions they require are the same as those for ferns.

S. kraussiana is a low creeper, perfect for terrariums. *S. emmeliana* is an erect-growing plant. *S. willdenovii* is a vigorous climber with unusual blue leaves, while *S. apus* is a trailer, good for hanging baskets.

73

SENSITIVE PLANT *(Mimosa pudica)*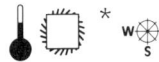

This is a fascinating plant for both adults and children, because its delicate and feathery leaves and petioles droop and fold up instantly (and temporarily) whenever it is touched or even if a lighted match is held close to it. Plants may be grown easily from seeds, which are often available in stores. It becomes leggy and rank after about a year, but it is not difficult to grow more plants at any time. It is very sensitive to mealybugs.

SILK OAK *(Grevillea robusta)*

This is a pleasant plant with graceful and feathery foliage similar to that of the false aralia. It will grow to three feet in height. Silk oak likes cool and moist conditions and can spend the summer outdoors with benefit in northern states. It does tend to become leggy if unchecked, so the growing tips should be cut back regularly, under the no-time gardener's policy of preventive pruning. Silk oak will do poorly if its soil becomes dry.

SNAKE PLANT *(Sansevieria)*

The snake plant is actually a succulent, but few of us think of it as such, and so we include it among the foliage plants. It has long been very popular probably because of its great tolerance to adverse conditions. It is also called mother-in-law tongue and bowstring. Like the cast iron plant, *Sansevieria* can grow perfectly well in hot, dry, and dim locations (including, it seems, most old hotel lobbies in the country). It is slow growing and tough—a perfect plant for the no-time gardener.

Sansevieria's thick, sword-shaped, usually upright leaves grow to eighteen inches or more in height, but in some vari-

---

*Prefers dry soil but high room humidity.

eties hug the ground. It is propagated easily by division of the rootstock or by taking a leaf cutting. (Be careful not to turn the leaf cutting upside-down when setting it in the rooting medium, for roots grow only from the downward portion of the cutting.)

Many varieties of snake plant are available:

Variegated snake plant *(S. trifasciata laurenti)* has handsome yellow bands along its leaf margins. *S. trifasciata* is similar in form but without the yellow bands. Dwarf Congo snake plant *(S. trifasciata laurenti* 'compacta') has shorter leaves and yellow margins. Hahn's dwarf snake plant *(S. trifasciata* 'hahni') has light and dark green bands along the leaves.

There are many other interesting variegated varieties of this old standby.

SPATHE FLOWER *(Spathiphyllum)*

Here is an easy-to-grow, tough plant, suitable for the homes of no-time indoor gardeners. It has sword-shaped, glossy, green leaves. White blossoms will sometimes surprise you in the winter, but do not depend on their appearance. Two popular species are *S. clevelandii* and *S. floribundum.*

SPIDER PLANT
(Chlorophytum comosum)

Spider plant is one of the most popular house plants. Its grassy leaves, variegated cream and green in color, arch gracefully from either pot or hanging basket. Mature plants produce perfectly formed baby plants on the ends of long runners that resemble spiders hanging from a thread. Propagation is simply a matter of rooting one of the "baby spiders" in a rooting medium. The spider plant can store water in its tubers and can take dry soil for a fairly long time because of this characteristic. It is easy to care for and can take a fair amount of inattention—a good plant for the no-time indoor gardener.

STRAWBERRY GERANIUM
(Saxifraga sarmentosa)

This trailing plant, also called strawberry begonia and mother of thousands, is good for both hanging baskets and terrariums. All it really asks is a woodsy soil, containing plenty of organic matter, and a cool location. Leaves of the strawberry geranium resemble those of the true geranium, and it sends out runners just as strawberry plants do. The leaves of the standard variety are deep olive in color with silver gray markings. An interesting variant, *S. sarmentosa* 'tricolor,' has dark green leaves marked with white and pink and is considerably more difficult to grow. Strawberry geranium can easily be harmed by overfertilization.

SWEET FLAG *(Acorus gramineus)*

Here is a moisture-loving plant that grows only two inches tall. It is a pleasant little fellow and will be most happy in a terrarium.

SYNGONIUM
See Arrowhead.

TI PLANT *(Cordyline terminalis)*

C. terminalis is only one of many species of *Cordyline*, but it is certainly the most popular. Also called firebrand, it will last for only one to three years and grow to two feet in height before dying out, but its spectacular young life is certainly worth your placing this plant on the list of house plant candidates. It has long, upward-reaching leaves of cerise, purple, and green, which grow from a cane trunk. Another popular species is *C. australis*, which features long and slender leaves. The ti plant is very popular in Hawaii, where its colorful leaves are used in making grass skirts. It is sold there in tourist shops as "ti log." In recent years breeders have developed variations of the original plant, including a dwarf and a variegated variety, which are sold under various names.

UMBRELLA SEDGE
(Cyperus alternifolius)

This popular exotic plant has narrow, pointed, grasslike leaves that grow in clusters. It will grow up to two feet tall in a pot. Constant moisture is essential, and propagation is a simple matter of root division.

Related species include *C. papyrus*, similar in appearance and requirements but which grows to seven feet in height over the years, and a dwarf variety, *C. alternifolius gracilis.*

VELVET PLANT *(Gynura)*

This is a vigorous-growing plant with dark red, velvety leaves. It will offer a fine contrast to your green plants. It is best to train velvet plant to some support, to keep it in bounds, although the no-time gardener will want to practice frequent preventive pruning in order to encourage bushiness. Nevertheless, the plants tend to become spindly and leggy with age and should not be counted on for the long run.

There are two common varieties—*G. aurantiaca*, which is upright in growth habit, and *G. sarmentosa*, a smaller and loosely twining plant. The flowers of both have a disagreeable scent and should be removed immediately after they bloom. The plant also tends to harbor mealybugs.

WANDERING JEW *(Tradescantia)*

Tradescantia and *Zebrina* both claim the common name of Wandering Jew, and the two genera are so similar that they are commonly interchanged. They are easy to grow, tolerant, and vigorous trailers, which make them perfect for hanging baskets. Feed them regularly for good growth, less often for controlled growth. Propagation is simplicity itself. Take cuttings of growing tips and root them in water.

There are very many interesting species of this plant. *T. fluminensis*, the original Wandering Jew, has silver markings, but there are many variants of different markings and colors available today. *T. albiflora* has bluish green leaves with white stripes. *Z. pendula* is an excellent house plant whose leaves have purple undersides. Again, there are several interesting variegated varieties.

YEW *(Podocarpus)*

Yews are prized outdoor plants in many parts of the country but can be made into attractive house plants anywhere. These hardy evergreens can provide welcome contrast to your tropicals. They are slow growing and tolerant of adverse conditions. They will take low temperatures without a whimper and might require more than the usual amount of pruning to keep them in an attractive shape. Although slow in growing, they will keep on growing and will require repotting from time to time.

Southern yew *(P. macrophylla angustifolia)* is a vigorous grower that responds well to pruning. Other similar species include *P. macrophylla* 'Nagai' and *P. macrophylla* 'Maki.'

Flowering House Plants

In nature nearly all the plants mentioned in this book produce flowers. In this chapter, however, we will confine our attention to those that can reasonably be expected to produce attractive blossoms under home conditions with fair regularity. These are, in other words, plants that are grown indoors for their blossoms rather than their foliage.

The flowering house plants, of which there are thousands, comprise many families and have a very wide range of cultural requirements. Those native to warm regions will grow readily under home conditions, and those from temperate regions demand cool temperatures, especially at night. Some are spring- and summer-flowering plants that we will force into bloom in midwinter. And still others have such attractive foliage that they are grown for this beauty alone; their flowers are an added bonus.

The plants and plant groups selected for individual attention in the following pages are those that are both attractive and easy, or fairly easy, to grow. Many of the most beautiful plants seen in greenhouses, including some that fairly blaze with hundreds of colorful blossoms, will soon wilt and die in your care, simply because no average home can possibly match the special conditions offered by a greenhouse. Further, the florist has learned the subtle art of manipulation of both light and special chemicals to force plants to flower at certain times of the year. Such plants are not included in this chapter.

Two requirements of flowering house plants deserve your special consideration. First, these plants in order to flower need plenty of light, especially in the winter and during the period of flower formation. Second, most of them require very cool night temperatures—as low as 50° and certainly not over 60°. If you cannot meet these requirements, then you must choose your flowering plants with great care, or learn to be happy with foliage plants, cacti, and succulents.

On to the flowering house plants:

ACHIMENES

This plant, grown from a rhizome planted in March, April, or May, produces petunialike blossoms of red or blue, which appear in the summer. Its rambling nature makes it perfect for hanging baskets, and it will be happy on porch or patio as well as indoors. Give *Achimenes* a sunny window but some protection from the sun during the scorching days of summer. After its flowering period has finished, allow the entire plant to dry, and then store the rhizome in its pot, or in sand, at 50° to 60°, watering only if the rhizome begins to wither. The foliage of this plant is handsome, also, providing an extra bonus.

AFRICAN VIOLET

The African violet, a low-growing member of the gesneriad (gloxinia) family, is certainly the most popular flowering house plant and is possibly the most popular of all house plants. Its virtues are both simple and irresistible: It is easy to grow, and its blossoms are both attractive and profuse.

This plant does have special requirements that, although

not difficult to provide, are essential to success. It likes a warm temperature—68° to 75°—which happens to be the range of many warmer homes (and which also might explain why the African violet seems to be the favorite plant of everybody's elderly aunt). It likes good light (but no long periods of direct sun), moderate to high humidity, and a constantly moist (but not soggy) soil. Its soil should be humusy, with a high percentage of peat or other organic matter. (Most suppliers, even supermarkets, offer potting soil for African violets.) In watering, be sure not to splash the foliage without drying it thoroughly afterward (since standing water droplets on leaves causes spotting). The leaves should, however, be washed regularly in a mild soap solution, after which they should be rinsed thoroughly and allowed to dry in the shade. Last, avoid chilling the plant, either with air or water. Temperatures should never go below 60°, and cold water should never be used. Follow these rules and your chances with an African violet should be good indeed.

There are so many varieties of this plant that we will not attempt to select any for inclusion here. There are both single- and double-flowered varieties in various shades of red, pink, blue, lavender, purple, and white. There are also some handsome bicolored varieties.

African violets rarely need repotting—certainly not more than once every two years and then only to a pot one size larger. Some can go for much longer periods without repotting. Supplemental light during the evening hours does help the plants to attain greater vigor, especially during the short days of autumn and winter. Be advised, also, that unglazed clay pots are not the best choice for African violets, since the bottom leaves, resting on the lips of moist pots, can easily rot. Use plastic or glazed ceramic pots, or dip the rims of unglazed pots in paraffin before using them.

Propagation of African violets is simple with leaf cuttings. Root your favorite varieties, and in a year or so you will have some dandy Christmas presents for family and friends.

AMARYLLIS

Here is a bulb plant that is perfect for indoor growing. In the dead of winter, it produces spectacular trumpet-shaped blossoms, borne in a cluster on top of a twelve- to eighteen-inch stalk. The blossoms are of very good size and are available in a variety of colors—white, red, pink, or orange.

It is difficult to fail with amaryllis. Many bulbs are sold prepotted, so judicious watering is your only responsibility. If you buy unpotted bulbs, however, be sure to select a very small pot, with a diameter no larger than three inches greater than the bulb itself. Use humusy soil, setting the bulb firmly so that from one-half to two-thirds of it is *above* the soil line (or plant according to the grower's directions). October to March is the usual potting time. The plant should be placed in maximum sunlight, and the soil should be kept moist but not soggy. The stalk should grow vigorously and produce blossoms within two months.

After the blossoms have faded, cut the flower stalk, but do not disturb the leaves (which must produce food that the plant will use for next year's blossoming). When the danger of spring frost has passed, sink the pot in soil outdoors. Bring it back in before the first autumn frost and let it dry out in a cool basement until after New Year's Day. Then repot the bulb in fresh soil, and resume watering for new blossoms. For blooming around Christmas, bring the plant indoors about the first of August, remove the bulb from its pot and let it dry for eight to ten weeks. Then repot it, move it to a sunny spot, and resume watering.

BEGONIA

There are more than six thousand varieties of this popular plant, many of which produce both showy and colorful leaves and beautiful blossoms. So loved are these plants that some growers deal in them exclusively, and many home enthusiasts find time for no other indoor plants. Begonias may be temperamental in their requirements, although your chances of success will be improved greatly, if you choose the right varieties to begin with. They will, depending on the variety, grow from six to eighteen inches in height.

Tuberous begonias are good for porches and terraces but not as house plants. Rex begonias have spectacular foliage and, again, are fine outdoors but not indoors.

Wax begonias will do well either indoors or outdoors and are not difficult to raise in either place. They like full sun in the winter and partial shade during the heat of summer. Give them a constantly moist soil and warmer-than-average temperatures. (But do remember that they might not flower if autumn and winter night temperatures are over 70°.)

Fibrous-rooted begonias are the largest group of all and are by far the best house plants of this far-flung family. Scores of varieties are commonly available, including many that flower constantly and profusely. Many tumble freely from hanging baskets. Their culture is similar to that recommended for wax begonias. Most florists and greenhouses can show you a variety of fibrous-rooted begonias, among which you can select a favorite for experimentation in your home.

BROMELIADS

There are some attractive flowering varieties in this large family of plants. However, since most of the bromeliads are grown for their attractive foliage rather than their flowers, they are treated under foliage plants in Chapter 3.

CALLA LILY (Zantedeschia)

Here is an outdoor favorite that can be grown as a house plant, too. Of the two common varieties, the white lily should be planted in August, the yellow lily in November. Both will continue to grow and blossom continually; but unless they are given a dormant period in summer, the blossoms will become smaller and smaller.

Plant the rhizomes at a temperature of 60° to 65°. After growth has started, move the plants to a cooler location— 55° to 60°. (The white varieties like a cool night temperature; the yellow ones can take a warmer night temperature.) Start the dormant period in June by withholding water, giving them none at all, unless the rhizomes begin to shrivel. In August or November, repot the rhizomes and resume watering for new blooming.

CHENILLE PLANT *(Acalypha hispida)*

This member of the spurge family has deep red and trailing flowers that appear in summer. Humidity is important for the heavy production of flowers. The main drawback to the chenille plant is its tendency to draw spider mites. Watch for them, because they can affect your other plants as well.

FLOWERING MAPLE *(Abutilon)*

This group of old-fashioned plants offers several good varieties. Its foliage is so attractive (maple-shaped and variegated) and its flower production unpredictable enough to cause many enthusiasts to grow these plants for their foliage alone. With proper treatment, however, you will be rewarded with beautiful bell-shaped flowers in shades of red, orange, yellow, or white. Light and moisture are both crucially important for good blooming.

Flowering maple can be grown from seeds planted in spring, or from cuttings made any time. Root the cuttings in water or a sterile medium. These plants, which were favorites of our great-grandfathers, are still popular today.

GERANIUM *(Pelargonium)*

These are common and popular plants for patio and window box production, and they can be successful indoors, too, if the rules are followed. Critical to vigorous growth and profuse blossoming are full sun and cool temperatures. The ideal night temperatures for geraniums range from 55° to 60°, while warmer night conditions can inhibit flowering. Since the geranium's foliage is susceptible to rot, do not let water stand on the leaves.

There are several large groups of geraniums. The best for indoor production, however, are the varieties of *Pelargonium hortorum*, sometimes called the "house group" or zonal geraniums, of which there are hundreds.

You may start either by buying potted specimens from your plant dealer or by begging cuttings from friends. The cuttings are rooted quite easily in a sterile rooting medium and may soon be potted. If you want flowers in winter, take cuttings in May and start them immediately. Pot the plants as soon as vigorous roots have formed, and pinch off all flower buds until mid-autumn in order to encourage foliage growth. If, however, you want flowers in the spring and summer—perhaps with the idea of moving the plants to porch or patio—then begin the same process in October.

GLOXINIA *(Sinningia speciosa)*

After the African violet, the gloxinia is certainly the most popular member of the gesneriad family. It is low growing, no more than ten inches in height, with large velvety leaves and large bell-shaped flowers in shades of violet, red, pink, and white, including many bicolored and double-blossomed varieties. It is a good plant for either outdoor or indoor culture.

Gloxinia likes warm temperatures, moist soil, and especially good air circulation for good health. It grows from tubers, which are generally started in midwinter. After the plant has finished flowering (about four months after planting), dry out the plant thoroughly, then store the tuber in its pot or in sand, in cool temperatures (around 55°). Water the tuber only enough to keep it from withering. In February or March repot the tuber in fresh soil and resume watering and warm

85

temperatures. In four months another round of spectacular blooming should take place. Gloxinia is more susceptible than most plants to a number of insect pests.

GOLDFISH PLANT *(Columnea)*

The goldfish plant is so-called because its tubular flowers, in bright shades of red, pink, orange, or yellow, resemble the fantail goldfish. Some varieties are vinelike in growth and are perfect for hanging baskets. Others have very pretty variegated foliage. The cultural requirements are the same as those for African violets. Propagation from stem cuttings is simple.

ITALIAN BELLFLOWER *(Campanula isophylla)*

This attractive plant, often mistakenly called star of Bethlehem, is good for hanging baskets because of its trailing nature. Like many flowering house plants, it needs plenty of moisture and cool night temperatures for maximum production of blossoms. It is short lived and is best treated as a summer annual.

SHRIMP PLANT *(Beloperone guttata)*

The flower of this unusual plant does, indeed, resemble the shape of a shrimp. It tends to become leggy in growth, and so it should be pinched back often in order to encourage bushy growth and a height of about twelve inches. The shrimp plant will appreciate a summer outdoors, but it should be pruned back severely beforehand. It is more difficult to grow than most plants included here, although some people appear to have no trouble at all with it.

WAX PLANT *(Hoya carnosa)*

Here is an old favorite and a vigorous grower. It has waxy

leaves, variegated in some varieties, and alluring flowers in yellow, pink, or white, all of which have a very nice scent. *H. carnosa variegata* has white leaf margins but is only representative of the many variegated varieties that have interesting markings in white, green, pink, cream, yellow, or silver. The wax plant is another that is grown as much (and sometimes more) for its foliage as for its flowers. Good dwarf varieties include *H. bella*, *H. minima*, and *H. lacunosa*. Rope hoya *(H. carnosa compacta)* has an unusual leaf shape.

Wax plants are suitable for either pots (although some will need support) or hanging baskets. Keep them on the dry side, especially during their autumn rest period. They seem to bloom better when slightly pot-bound. Take care not to injure the long shoots produced each season. Pruning these will cost a season of flowers.

ZEBRA PLANT *(Aphelandra squarrosa)*

It is difficult to decide whether to grow this plant for its sparkling foliage (which contrasts clear white veins on bright green leaves) or its cheerful yellow flowers that appear in the autumn. Either is certainly worth the growing of the zebra plant and is well worth giving close attention to its requirements. A moist environment is especially important; if your home cannot provide humidity during winter, try the plant in a terrarium. It seldom is attractive after three years, but cuttings are made easily. Prune the plant rather severely after its fall blooming period and decrease its water supply over the winter. The plant tends to lose its lower leaves quite readily.

FORCING SPRING BULBS

A most pleasant way to enjoy a touch of spring in the dead of winter is to force spring-flowering bulbs for indoor bloom. Tulips, hyacinths, daffodils and other *narcissi*, crocus, grape hyacinths, lily-of-the-valley, scilla—all can be coaxed into fragrant and colorful bloom during the gray days of January,

BULBS IN A FORCING PAN

February, and March. In fact, many of us in the northern reaches of the country depend on these harbingers to convince ourselves that, yes, spring really *will* come, and it will be as glorious as ever.

The prerequisites for bulb forcing include special bulb pans (which are nothing more than shallow clay pots, available at any garden center), a suitable soil mixture, a proper place for cool and dark storage of the potted bulbs, and a little special attention.

Selecting Bulbs

Hyacinths are the easiest of all bulbs to force, while tulips are the most difficult. The rest should present no great problems if you bear in mind the rules. If you are attempting the process for the first time, however, start with hyacinths. Table 2 will suggest the varieties of each plant most suited to indoor forcing, although you should also depend on the advice of a nurseryman whom you trust. In general choose the largest and most perfectly formed bulbs. Since you will not be buying a large quantity for indoor use, you might as well pay a little extra for top quality. See that the paper-thin skin is intact and that the bottom of the bulb, from which the roots will grow, has not been injured. If you are buying a large number of bulbs for planting outdoors, save some of the best for your indoor project.

Storage Before Potting

If you will not be potting the bulbs immediately, store them at 55° to 63° in a location with good ventilation. If they begin to shrivel from dryness, moisten them daily with a plant mister. The actual potting process should take place no earlier than October 1 and no later than December 1. Earlier potting, of course, means earlier bloom.

Potting

The potting soil for bulbs should be low in nutrients and high in drainage capacity. A good mixture is three parts garden loam, two parts peat moss, and one part builder's sand. Do not add compost or manure, since nothing will be gained in doing so (the bulbs already hold all the nutrients the plant will need), and rotting can become a problem.

To help both drainage and ventilation of the root system, put some broken crockery in the bottom of the bulb pan, being certain to place one piece directly over the drainage hole—not to seal it but to prevent soil from being washed out of the pot. Then fill the pan partially with the potting mixture, set the bulbs firmly but gently on top, and work more potting mixture around the bulbs until only the tips show. In the end, the soil should come to one-fourth inch to one inch from the top of the pan, depending on its size. At least one inch of soil should be used; a great amount more is not needed.

Bulbs may be spaced as closely together as you wish, as long as they do not touch each other. Tulip bulbs have a flat side that should be pressed against the side of the pan. Working around the pan in this manner, you can plant six to nine bulbs in a six-inch pan, including one in the middle.

Water the potting mixture thoroughly after planting, and label each pot with the specific name of the bulbs and the planting date. Your bulbs are now ready for the most important step—the winter sleep.

Table 2. RECOMMENDED BULBS FOR INDOOR FORCING

Tulips (to bloom in January and February)

Red: Bing Crosby, Cassini, Cellini, Charles, Christmas Marvel, Olaf, Paul Richter, Prominence, Topscore, Trance

Yellow: Bellona, Levant

White: Pax, Snow Star

Salmon: Apricot Beauty

Variegated: Kees Nelis, Madame Spoor, Merry Widow, Roland

Pink: Blenda, Preludium

Tulips (to bloom in March and April)

Red: Albury, Cardinal, Couleur, Danton, Robinea

Yellow: Makassar, Ornament, Yellow Present

White: Blizzard

Orange: Orange Sun

Variegated: Carl M. Bellman, Denbola, Edith Eddy, Golden Eddy, Paris

Pink: Palestrina, Peerless Pink, Pink Supreme, Rose Beauty, Virtuoso

Hyacinths (to bloom in January and February)

Red: Amsterdam, Jan Bos

Pink: Anna Marie, Delight, Eros, Lady Derby, Princess Irene

Blue: Bismark, Delft Blue, Ostara

White: Edelweiss, L'Innocense, Madame Kruger

Hyacinths (to bloom in March and April)

Red: Amsterdam

Pink: Eros, Lady Derby, Marconi, Pink Pearl, Princess Irene

Blue: Blue Giant, Blue Jacket, Marie, Ostara

White: Carnegie, Colesseum

Daffodils (to bloom in January and February)
    Carleton, Golden Harvest, King Alfred
Daffodils (to bloom in March and April)
    Cheerfulness, Geranium, Gold Medal, Rembrandt, Van
    Sion
Crocuses (to bloom from January through April)
    Grand Maitre, Joan of Arc, Peter Pan, Pickwick, Re-
    membrance

Richard E. Widmer, *Care of House Plants*, Agricultural Extension Service, University of Minnesota, Extension Bulletin 274, rev. 1970, p. 24. Based on studies conducted at Michigan State University.

Winter Sleep

Outdoors in your yard, spring-flowering bulbs spend the winter in cold, dark storage. They are not inactive in their outdoor sleep, however; they are sending out vigorous white roots, while the snow flies above, in preparation for their great spring fling. Indoors you must recreate this winter sleep to give the bulbs a chance to develop roots. If you provide temperatures that are too warm, the bulbs will be triggered into premature and stunted growth.

The winter sleeping location will depend on the climate in your area and any supplemental refrigeration you can provide. The temperature should be no lower than 35° and no higher than 50°. Hyacinths can take a higher temperature —up to 55°—with no apparent harm. Northerners, who can depend on crisp autumn weather, might start by storing the potted bulbs on a back porch, moving them later to an unheated garage and, when the temperatures dip below freezing, to a cool part of a basement. Record the temperatures in several locations around the house and move the plants accordingly. If the weather does not cooperate, you can store them in a refrigerator, which should provide the proper temperature constantly. In any case, keep the bulbs out of strong light and keep the soil moist. Total darkness is fine, and the occasional light from a refrigerator bulb will do no harm. On a porch or another open location protection from light can be provided in many different ways. An inverted pot placed on top of the bulb pan will do the trick. Or the pots may be set in a box and covered with sand. A closed box is fine. Soil moisture may be retained if you seal off air from the potted bulbs. Enclosing them in a dark green plastic trash bag is an effective and simple method. Or they may be covered with sand, which should be kept just slightly moist. In a refrigerator they can be watered occasionally. However you choose to provide these conditions, it is essential that the potted bulbs receive relative darkness, cool temperatures, and adequate soil moisture.

In about six weeks the bulbs should begin to send out roots. In a minimum of twelve weeks from the time of potting, or as long as twenty, they should be ready to emerge from the bulb pan.

Active Growth

When the root system is well developed, and a white growing tip is evident, the bulb is ready to be brought out into the open for active growth. As a test, knock out the soil ball from one pan and examine the roots. If they are strong and vigorous, covering the bottom of the soil ball in a thick mat, you may be sure the plant is ready.

At this time place the plant in an open location, out of direct sun, at a temperature of 50° to 60°. Be especially careful to keep hyacinths in a very dim location for the first few days to encourage the flower stalk to make rapid upward growth. The need for cool temperatures during this stage will again dictate a storage place. You might find that an unheated sun porch or a north window of a basement is ideal. In warmer parts of the country an open breezeway might do, if shade is provided.

After the growing tip has changed from white to green, the plant may be moved into a sunny location and given a slightly warmer temperature—up to 65° during the day and 5° to 10° cooler at night. Many people simply transfer the pots from the north to the south basement windows. Be sure to keep the soil well watered during this entire period.

After the buds are nearly ready to open, the pans may be brought to the place where you want them to bloom. Keep them well watered until the plants have finished their colorful performance.

The only drawback to the entire process of forcing bulbs is that the bulbs often cannot be reused. Some people do let the plants turn yellow, then dry the bulbs, and plant them outdoors in the fall. But these bulbs rarely produce well again, because we have tampered with their biological time clocks. But since any bulb has a life-span of only a few years anyway, most of us feel that one brilliant indoor performance is enough for any bulb to provide.

CARE OF GIFT PLANTS

Most commercially produced flowering gift plants should be regarded as nothing more than long-lasting cut flowers. After the plant has stopped flowering, it should be thrown away. Most of these, including *Chrysanthemum*, azaleas, cyclamen, and primroses, are suitable only for outdoor culture. Some can be planted outdoors after they have bloomed, provided that they are varieties hardy in your area. Others, including azaleas and poinsettias, make good indoor–outdoor plants that can provide pleasure year after year, given proper care. Here is a rundown of some of the more popular flowering gift plants:

AZALEA

You may keep a potted azalea blooming for two months or more if you give it cool temperatures, diffused sunlight, and plenty of water. After it has stopped blooming, continue to

water the plant frequently and keep it in a bright location. In May after all danger of frost has passed, transplant the azalea into the open garden, giving it an acid soil. Prune it moderately around June 1. Before the first autumn frost, repot the plant, again giving it acid soil, and keep it in a very cool and light location for at least a month. An unheated sun porch or a cold frame is usually ideal for this purpose. During November bring the plant indoors. With cool temperatures and diffused sunlight the plant should bloom again in six to ten weeks.

CHRYSANTHEMUM

Most potted *Chrysanthemum* that come from florists cannot be replanted outdoors in northern areas, because they are varieties suited to the south; killing northern frosts will arrive in autumn before the plants have had a chance to bloom. As house plants, however, they are long-lasting and most beautiful. Keep them in your sunniest window at a temperature of 60° to 70°, and give them plenty of water. If you do receive a hardy variety (your florist might be able to advise you), give it a dormant period after it has bloomed. Then cut it back severely, and replant it outdoors in spring. You will have no guarantee of success, but it might be worth a try.

CYCLAMEN

There is no practical way to preserve this plant after it has finished flowering indoors. However, the flowering period can be prolonged greatly if room temperatures are held between 50° and 55°. Admittedly at temperatures such as these your cyclamen's pleasure will be your personal discomfort. Perhaps, though, you have an unheated sun porch with a window opening into the living room, where the plant can be displayed effectively. At warmer temperatures the blossoms will last probably for no more than two weeks. In any case keep the plant in a bright spot, and do not let water stand in the crown of the plant because of the probability of rot.

EASTER LILY

This hardy plant can be transplanted outdoors after it has bloomed but with no guarantee of success. After you receive the plant, keep it in bright light, water liberally every day, and try to keep the night temperatures down to 55° to 60°. Although most people simply discard the plant after it has finished blooming, you may try to return it to natural conditions. Keep watering the plant after it has bloomed, until the leaves have turned yellow. After the danger of spring frost has passed, plant the bulb in the garden under six to eight inches of soil. New growth should appear by summer, and the plant might even bloom again by autumn. More likely, however, the next flowers will appear during the following summer, which is the normal blooming time for the Easter lily.

HYDRANGEA

This plant, like the azalea, can be given special treatment to enable its return the following winter. Give your gift plant plenty of water and a bright spot out of direct sun. After it has finished blooming indoors, cut back the stems to within five inches of the soil line. After danger of frost has passed, sink the pot directly into the garden, in partial shade, and water it often during the season. In late August, repot it in a slightly larger pot with fresh soil. Just before the first frost (watch the weather forecast) bring the hydrangea inside for its dormant period. Store it in a cool (35° to 40°), dark place, and give it just enough water to prevent the stem from drying out. Right after New Year's Day remove any leaves that have not fallen off during dormancy, and move the plant to a sunny window. It should then be given cool to moderate temperatures. Start it out at 55° for the first few weeks; then increase its temperature to 60° to 65°. Give it a good dose of an all-purpose fertilizer at this time.

Some hydrangeas act as litmus paper. Their flowers will be blue if the soil is very acid and pink if it is only slightly acid.

POINSETTIA

A newly arrived poinsettia, like most other gift plants, should be given plenty of water, a cool room, and full sun. The colored bracts (they are not actually flowers) should last for three weeks at 70°, up to two months at 55° to 60°.

Since the leaves of the poinsettia are attractive, many people simply keep them as foliage plants, making no attempt to induce flowering the following year. They will do perfectly well as such, given ample water and diffused sunlight. If you want flowers to be produced the next year, however, there is a special procedure to follow:

After the bracts of the gift plant have fallen, move the plant to a cool basement or sun porch, where it will get plenty of light. Withhold water, giving it just enough to prevent complete dryness, and the plant will enter its dormant period. Around May 1, cut the plant back to within six inches of the soil line, and repot it in fresh soil. Resume watering at this time. If night temperatures will not go below 60°, you may place the pot outdoors for the summer, protecting the plant from very strong sunlight. When night temperatures again drop below 60°, move the plant indoors to a sunny, well-ventilated location.

If you want the poinsettia to bloom for Christmas, begin special treatment on October 1. At that time be sure that the plant receives a night temperature of 60° and a day temperature of 68° to 70°. Give the plant exactly fourteen hours of darkness every day from October 1 until the Christmas blooming period. In some parts of the country this will mean providing artificial darkness during the latter part of each day (such as moving the plant into a closet at a certain time) and providing supplemental light later on in the autumn, as the days grow shorter. Providing the extra light is simple with a twenty-four-hour timer attached to an artificial light source. Adjust it every few days. Admittedly this is a bothersome procedure, especially when it is so much easier to buy a blooming plant from a florist, but some enthusiasts take up the challenge each year as a matter of pride.

PRIMROSE *(Primula)*

A primrose may become a part of your permanent outdoor garden, after it has served indoors. When the blossoms have faded, move the plant to a cool basement and withhold water until spring, when the plant may be cut back severely, watered, and planted outside. Only *P. obconica* may be carried over to a second year indoors. After *P. obconica* has finished flowering, move it to a cool place and withhold water, forcing it to enter a dormant state. Water only enough to keep the soil from drying out completely. Then in autumn it may be repotted, placed in full sunlight, and watered freely. All primroses do best in full sunlight and cool night temperatures.

Cacti and Other Succulents

Many house plant fanciers are completely indifferent to cacti and the other succulents, and some express a distinct dislike for them. Still others are completely enthralled with these unusual and diverse plants, giving them attention to the exclusion of all others.

Whatever your individual preferences, there is no denying that the succulents (and cacti are but one group of succulents) are remarkably colorful and interesting subjects, easy to care for, and responsive to special attention. They are, further, ideal plants for the no-time gardener, since they require less attention than other plants. Most succulents ask little more than a sunny window, occasional water, and very occasional fertilizing. There is no pruning, no tying up, no staking, no repotting. They are slow growing and thoroughly dependable.

There are literally thousands of species in this plant category, including more than two thousand cacti alone. Of these, several hundred, both attractive and suitable for indoor culture, are bred and sold as house plants.

Although cacti are succulent plants, the two are treated as separate groups in common practice, and in these pages we will follow that practice. Botanists classify cacti according to their flower characteristics, although most of us recognize them because of the unusual physical properties they have developed in surviving the demanding climates of their native habitats. The leaves of desert cacti (xerophytes) have evolved into sharp and hard spines that grow from small tufts of hair called areoles. Their stems have become enormously swollen and enlarged, which enables the plant to hold stores of water. Quite a different cactus group are the forest cacti (epiphytes), which come to us from the mountains of Brazil, where they live in the crotches of trees. They have no spines, but their inaccessibility to ground water has forced them to develop elongated stems. The Christmas cactus *(Zygocactus)* is the best known of the epiphytes.

The succulents are similar to the cacti in many basic characteristics, but they have no areoles. By far the best known of the succulents is the ubiquitous snake plant *(Sansevieria)*, which is commonly considered as one of the foliage plants and is discussed above. Among the hundreds of other house plant succulents are an amazing array of shapes, sizes, colors, and flowering characteristics, including some of the most unusual plants to be found in domestication. Here we find the fascinating *Lithops*, which looks for all the world like stones. Growing no more than two inches high, it produces beautiful yellow and white flowers that are larger than the plants themselves. *Euphorbias obesa*, on the other hand, grows into the form of a rust and green ball with perfectly regular markings. (If you don't like *E. obesa*, there are more than two thousand other *Euphorbias* to consider.) Elk's horn *(Rhombophyllum nelii)* bears a close resemblance to its common namesake and then leaps out of character by producing the most exquisite, daisylike flowers. Certainly every house plant grower can find among the succulents' dazzling array of plant form and color one that will bring beauty to the home and pleasure to the grower.

CARE OF CACTI AND SUCCULENTS

The secrets to success in raising cacti and succulents might very well be in exploding several myths that, if believed and acted upon, will retard the plants' development.

Myth number one says that cacti should rarely be watered. Believing this, many house plant growers virtually starve these poor plants into a state of retardation and total listlessness. In truth cacti should be watered nearly as liberally during their growing season as other plants. Only during autumn and winter, during the cacti's inactive period, should water be cut back severely. A good general rule is to soak the plants thoroughly and briefly twice a week during spring, summer, and early autumn, being sure to provide for fast and thorough drainage. Near the middle of fall, water not more than once every two weeks—less frequently, if you are working to produce blossoms the following summer—and continue this reduced amount until the latter part of March, when watering may be increased gradually until, by the middle of April, the twice-weekly schedule has been resumed.

Myth number two states that cacti rarely, if ever, need fertilization. In truth they will respond well to normal applications of plant food but only during their active growing period. (Some people, acting upon myths one and two, never realize that cacti *have* a growing period.)

The last myth says that cacti, since they are desert plants, require a hot and dry environment. Not true. While it is true that constantly damp and cool conditions will hurt these plants, cacti respond most favorably to a very cool atmosphere during the winter rest period (temperatures as low as 40°), and in summer they really don't care what the temperature is. You must remember that, in their native desert climates, daily temperatures in summer can have a spread of fifty degrees or more. Most experts recommend, for cacti's best health, winter resting temperatures of 45° to 50°, suggesting that a cool sun porch might make a fine wintering place for your cacti. During summer forget about temperature. More important are good ventilation and lots of sunshine. Cacti are among those plants that will do very well outdoors in the summer. (But do not expose them to long periods of direct sun immediately after their winter rest period in a shaded spot.)

Succulents require much the same conditions as cacti, but they do appreciate some protection from strong sunlight, if they are to show their true colors; and they will require a little more water during the winter. Like the cacti, they will appreciate a winter rest in cooler temperatures, as low as 50° and preferably not over 60°.

POTTING SOIL FOR CACTI

Although cacti and succulents should not be grown in pure sand, they do need a soil that will offer very good drainage. There are several good recipes, one calling for equal parts of commercial potting soil, builder's sand, and peat (with a moderate amount of bone meal) and another that substitutes compost for peat. Whichever you use, be sure to provide more sand than is called for in other potting soils, and don't neglect to provide pebbles or broken crockery in the bottom of the pot for good drainage. They do best in clay pots, where moisture can escape through the pot walls.

INTRODUCING THE CACTI

There are so many individual cactus species, and so much grafting of one species onto another, that we will here limit our survey to the larger groups of cacti. If you should become totally enamored of these plants, a trip to your public library will reveal at least several good books devoted exclusively to the group.

The prickly pears (Opuntia) are a large group, most of which have broad and flat joints. The best known of the group is bunny-ear cactus *(Opuntia microdasys)*, which does indeed resemble a series of bunny ears set one atop the other at odd angles.

The Cereeae constitute the largest of the cactus tribes incorporating hundreds of individual species. Best known among the Cereeae are the picturesque "candelabras," which were a stock item in every Hollywood western film of the 1930's. Another interesting member is the old-man cactus, which sports long white "hair." Actually several different species share this common name.

The Hylocereanae are climbers and crawlers that sometimes send out aerial roots like ivy. They produce the most beautiful flowers of all cacti and often bloom at night. The stems of the Hylocereanae are often weak and easy to break.

Another large group is the hedgehog cacti (Echinocereanae). They are prized by house plant growers, because they flower more readily, and at a younger age, than other cacti. One of the most popular is *Echinocereus fitchii*, found wherever cacti are sold, which produces beautiful pink flowers on plants as young as two years. *Rebutia* is very popular, too, and very numerous. It flowers easily, producing blossoms around the base of the plant.

The Echinocactanae are also called hedgehog cacti. They resemble the Echinocereanae, but the Echinocactanae send their blossoms forth from the tops of the growing tips rather than from the base of the plant. Depend on these two families for easy-flowering cacti.

The Coryphanthanae are distinguished from all other cacti in that they have large, protruding tubercles (wartlike knobs) over the entire surface of their stems. The largest genus in the Coryphanthanae family is *Mammillaria*, which exudes a watery or milky sap when pierced.

The forest cacti, including the prized Christmas cactus *(Zygocactus truncatus)*, live in tree crotches in the wild. They take to grafting quite readily and in fact are often grafted onto terrestrial rootstock in order to increase their vigor. Nevertheless, most Christmas cacti are not so grafted and will thus appreciate a loose-textured potting mixture that contains a large percentage of sphagnum moss or peat.

THE UNUSUAL SUCCULENTS

In many ways succulents are even more interesting than cacti. For one thing most have a most pleasant leaf and/or stem texture that the spines of a cactus cannot match. Many succulents are beautiful to feel (somewhat like a very smooth stone) as well as to look at. Here again the variety of color, form, and texture is nearly mind-boggling. There is certainly room for a few succulents in every house plant collection, the more so because they are easy to grow.

Aloe is very easy to grow and is distinguished by sharply pointed leaves that end in needlelike spines, almost like a cactus that has not finished its evolutionary process. Best known is *A. variegata*, a modest and rewarding plant.

Agave is another popular succulent group, many of whose members produce spectacular flowers. Best known in this group is century plant *(A. americana)*, a tolerant and attractive low-growing species.

The genus *Echeveria* forms a very large group of pleasant, if not spectacular, plants. Most have fleshy leaves that are very tidy in arrangement, and some flower quite freely. *Echeveria* are easy to grow and easy to propagate. Many varieties require no more for this purpose than cutting off a leaf and placing it on top of moist sand. Roots and plants soon will form.

Hawarthia is a small plant that comes in a wide variety of forms and textures. It is ideal for dish gardens.

Sempervivum comprises a most attractive group. Its tight rosettes form low mats of gorgeous color, indoors or out. Where the winters are not too severe, *Sempervivum* may be grown on the patio, if some protection can be offered when frost threatens. It needs much more light than most succulents, and so some artificial illumination might be necessary. But it is very rewarding if its special requirements can be met. Some varieties are hardy in the north.

Crassula forms another large family, offering plants in a wide variety of both colors and forms. Start with jade plant *(C. argentea)*, a popular species that is very attractive and easy to grow. On a thick, treelike stalk, it sets forth dark, thick, jade green leaves. Princess pine *(C. pseudolycopodioides)* is a freely growing plant with small, closely spaced, thick leaves. Like most *Crassula*, it is tidy in form and not difficult to grow. *C. perfossa* (necklace vine) has

103

thick, triangular leaves growing on vinelike stems. It is a carefree and rambling plant.

Kalanchoes are both attractive in appearance and easy to grow, although many are short lived, lasting no more than a year. Like most short-lived house plants, however, they are remarkably easy to propagate, so you should have no trouble in keeping your favorite varieties in constant supply. The best-known of the *Kalanchoes* is *K. blossfeldiana*, of which there are many varieties. They are often seen in stores at Christmas time going under many popular names, including vulcan plant. *K. blossfeldiana* produces a profusion of small red blossoms. These, contrasted with its dark green and leathery leaves, explain its Yuletide popularity. Also try mother of thousands *(K. diagremontiana)* and *K. tubiflora*, both of which produce young plants freely along the edges of their leaves. Propagation of these two plants involves no more than your placing a leaf on moist sand and weighting it down with several pebbles. The young plantlets can soon be separated and nursed along in flats or separate pots. There are several other good *Kalanchoes* available and also other varieties and subvarieties of the species mentioned above. For quick and sometimes spectacular results they are good succulents for any home.

The genus *Sedum* (stonecrop) includes more than three hundred fifty varieties. Many of these are low and slow growing (although some grow quite vigorously), making them perfect for dish gardens. One of the more interesting members of the family is *S. stahlii* (coral beads), which has small, beadlike leaves. These drop off regularly and can be rooted with little trouble.

These are perhaps the most popular groups of succulents. There are, of course, many more, including some to suit any taste and most growing conditions. Some of the more popular of these are crown of thorns *(Euphorbia splendens)*, hen and chickens *(Sempervivum tectorum)*, rosary vine *(Ceropegia woodii)*, deer's tongue *(Gasteria verrucosa)*, cushion aloe *(Hawarthia)*, and elephant bush *(Portulacaria afra)*. None is very difficult to grow.

 Special Indoor Gardens

Much of the fun of house plant growing revolves around special and unusual projects through which we can give full play to our imaginations and experimental natures. We can create a temporary miniature woodland scene in a terrarium or a colorful cactus garden in a soup bowl. We can grow beautiful house plants from kitchen scraps or plant lettuce on top of the refrigerator. By exercising our options more completely, by trying things we have never tried before, we gain a new sense of achievement. And with the aid of the new fluorescent lights made especially for plant growing, few of these special projects are beyond the capabilities of any house or apartment dweller.

DISH GARDENS AND PLANTERS

Attractive displays of several different plants may be created by arranging them in a dish garden or a planter. A dish garden should be used for low- and slow-growing plants, while larger ones may be grouped in a larger planter of nearly any size or shape.

Any shallow container may be used for a dish garden—a soup bowl, a baking dish, or an attractive ceramic planter designed for this purpose. It need not have a drainage hole, but it must be watertight and rustproof. First place a layer

of gravel to hold excess water in the bottom of the container. Charcoal is even better for this purpose, since it will keep the water fresh. Then place a layer of potting mixture on top, leaving one-half to three-fourths inch of room for watering. If you wish, you may add a thin layer of sand or colorful pebbles to enhance the final appearance of the dish garden. The trick is to choose low- and slow-growing plants—so that no one quickly dwarfs the others—and also plants that have similar cultural requirements. Good plants for dish gardens include boxwood, the smaller *Dracaena*, Irish moss (baby's tears), ivy, mother of thousands, *Pellionia*, *Peperomia*, *Pilea*, *Podocarpos*, wax plant, cacti, and smaller succulents. (Cacti and succulents, of course, should not be combined with plants that require higher soil moisture.)

Planters can be used for larger-growing plants of nearly any variety, as long as they, too, have similar cultural requirements. Some modern homes have built-in planters, often under picture windows, but you may construct one to fit anywhere in your home. It is best to keep plants in porous clay pots when adding them to a large planter, since most house plants react badly when they are given too much growing room. A good plan is to line the bottom of the planter with at least one inch of gravel, set the potted plants in the desired positions, and then fill in around them with sphagnum moss or peat moss. Smaller pots may be raised to the proper height with the aid of bricks or inverted pots. The plants may then be given the proper amount of moisture by adding water to the peat, letting the water soak through the clay pots. Plants may easily be added and removed, also, if they are kept in their individual pots. Plans for constructing planters are given in many larger indoor gardening books and in monthly magazines for home beautification. Make a thorough search of your local library's resources if you are interested in building a planter.

BOTTLE GARDENS AND TERRARIUMS

Our fascination with bottle gardens and terrariums is both universal and understandable. Here we can create a self-enclosed plant world in miniature, completely landscaped to our liking, with rocks, pebbles, perhaps an attractive piece of driftwood, and plants of varied color, texture, and form, all artfully and perfectly placed. In the humid atmosphere of the glass garden, we can easily grow plants that would not survive on our window sills. We can grow not only tropical plants but also native woodland varieties that would never tolerate the dry, artificial heat of the average home. The fascination of glass-enclosed gardens extends down to the youngest child, making this an enjoyable project for everyone in the family.

A further bonus for the no-time gardener is that glass gardens, once established, need less care than any other house plant environment. A terrarium establishes in itself a nearly perfect environment for the growing of tropical plants. They will need less water and less attention of all kinds. Here is truly a no-work way to grow those exotic plants that even your green-thumb friends will recognize as difficult specimens.

Any clear glass enclosure (colored glass will not do) will make a fine bottle garden or terrarium, as long as it has a removable top. Your options include ordinary bottles, aquariums, brandy snifters, apothecary jars, and old fish bowls. Bottles with narrow necks can present quite a challenge, not incomparable with that of building a ship in a bottle, but special tools can be purchased or devised at home to solve most problems of arranging plants in these close quarters.

The plants you choose to include in a glass garden should be low and slow growing and should have similar cultural requirements, since they will share the same environment. The three general groups of glass-garden plants are tropical plants, native woodland plants, and cacti and succulents. The members of any one group should never be mixed with the others. Of the three the woodland plants require a temperature of under 70°, while the other two should be maintained at 75° to 78° for best results. Cacti and succulents should have no cover, since they appreciate low humidity and good ventilation; they are not good subjects for bottle gardens but are ideal for terrariums.

Any glass garden should first have a bottom layer of gravel or charcoal to provide good drainage. After that, prepare a mixture of equal parts of potting soil, sand, and peat moss. (Cacti and succulents can take half again as much sand.) For a nice touch you may line the sides of the glass enclosure with moss, which you have dug from the woods, or sheet moss, which is available from most florists. Place the green side of the moss against the glass, and it will remain green as long as adequate moisture is given. Provide at least one and one-half inches of potting mixture but not so much that the open area of the enclosure is reduced to a point of aesthetic imbalance or that there will be inadequate room for top growth. To create extra interest form slopes and terraces with the soil, perhaps using flat stones for the special terracing effect. Arrange the plants with thoughtful care to create

the balanced effect you desire. In bottles long tweezers or photographer's tongs can be used for planting, and a cork attached to a slender stick is fine for tamping the soil.

After the plants have been arranged, there probably will be soil adhering to the sides of the glass. Wash this down with a plant sprayer; then water the entire garden, and put the top in place.

The glass garden should be kept in a bright spot but never in direct sunlight. Not only will the strong rays of the sun create temperatures far too high for any plant to stand (the so-called greenhouse effect), but in some cases a magnifying-glass effect can be created, bending the sun's rays in such a way to burn a plant instantly. The top of the glass garden should be kept on at all times, unless the glass becomes excessively fogged. Then the top should be removed until the fog disappears. Ideally the glass garden should be watered just enough so that excess fogging does not occur. The moisture that the plants release should enter the miniatmosphere and be recirculated by the plants, making frequent watering unnecessary.

Frequent pruning in the glass garden is a necessity, especially since the lush and tropical microenvironment will encourage many plants to grow wildly. Do not be afraid to cut back any terrarium plant at will. The only result will be a bushier and healthier plant. Again, in bottle gardens this chore will require a special pair of scissors, which can be found at some specialty houses and, if unavailable elsewhere, at medical supply houses. (The latter will be very expensive.)

Tropical plants for glass gardens include African violet, begonias, Chinese evergreen, *Coleus*, creeping fig, small *Dracaena*, *Fittonia*, grape ivy, Irish moss (ideal for ground cover), Joseph's coat, strawberry geranium, *Peperomia*, small *Philodendron*, snake plant, pothos, Wandering Jew.

Native woodland plants for glass gardens include bloodroot, dogtooth violet, Dutchman's breeches, evergreen seedlings, smaller ferns, ground pine, Jack-in-the-pulpit, juniper seedlings, maidenhair fern, money wort, moss (for ground cover), *Pipsissewa*, rattlesnake plantain, partridge berry, pitcher plant, violet, wild strawberry, wintergreen, other low-growing and attractive plants found growing in shaded areas.

Warning: Be sure of your state's regulations before picking any wild plants.

HOUSE PLANTS FROM KITCHEN SCRAPS

Turning kitchen wastes into house plants is an enjoyable family project and a most instructive one for children. The seeds, pips, stones, or tops of nearly all fruits and vegetables will germinate and grow under proper conditions. And even though few of them will make good permanent house plants, you can keep enough projects going around the kitchen to provide a continuing show.

The best seeds and pips for easy germination are those from tropical fruits, including oranges, lemons, grapefruits, limes, and pomegranates. In nature these germinate and grow in constantly warm temperatures similar to those found in your home. Seeds and pips of hardy plants, such as apples and pears, and the stones of cherries and apricots may not germinate until they have undergone a period of alternate freezing and thawing, such as they find in their natural environments. To satisfy this need you must carry out a process called stratification, in which the seeds are buried in a tray of moist sand and then placed in the refrigerator for four months, moving the tray back and forth between the freezing

compartment and the vegetable storage area every week or so. After that, they should be potted in a regular mixture, about one-half inch deep, and kept in cool temperatures until they have germinated. When green sprouts have shown, move the pots to a warmer place in full sunshine.

VEGETABLE TOPS

The tops of carrots, beets, turnips, and parsnips may be planted in moist potting soil or merely set in a saucer of water to produce interesting and attractive, albeit short-lived, house plants. Simply cut off the top inch of the vegetable, trim off any greens, pot it, and put it in a warm and sunny spot. New growth should begin within a week or two and should make quick progress after that.

A sweet potato can quickly produce a lush and vigorous vine that may be trained around a kitchen window. Simply place the narrowed end of a whole sweet potato (one that has several eyes on the upper portion) in a jar just wide enough to support the potato. Keep the water level of the jar high enough to cover only the bottom of the sweet potato. If you keep it in a warm and sunny spot, roots will soon grow into the water, and shoots will emerge from each of the eyes on top. The vine's progress will be quite rapid after that. The sweet potato has enough stored energy to keep the plant going for a long while without supplemental fertilizer. (The same thing can be done with other potatoes, although most of them prefer a cool, dark place for germination, after which they should be moved to a warmer and brighter spot.)

Some kitchen scraps may be turned into permanent and very attractive house plants. The most popular example is the avocado, which grows into a handsome tree indoors and can become very large over the years. Some others include the date palm, the pineapple, and the coffee tree.

AVOCADO

Wash the avocado stone in warm water, removing all the

brown skin. Suspend the stone in a jar of water, using galvanized nails (which serve better than toothpicks) if necessary for support and keeping the water level just high enough to cover the bottom of the stone. Place the jar in a warm, dim spot, watch the water level carefully, and change the water weekly to keep it fresh. The stone should split in from four to eight weeks, sending out roots below and a growing tip above. Move it to a brighter spot, now, still maintaining warm temperatures. After strong roots have formed and the first leaves have begun to show, pot the young plant in a mixture containing plenty of sand and keep it in a warm, sunny spot. Water the avocado only when the soil becomes dry.

DATE PALM

A date stone can be planted to produce a very attractive potted palm which can grow eventually to an impressive size. Begin with a good-sized stone from a fresh date. Plant it one-half inch deep in a regular potting mixture with plenty of sand. Keep the pot in a temperature range of 70° to 80° in a dim spot; it should germinate in about a month. After the first green shoots have appeared, move the pot to a bright location. Normal room temperatures should be good for the date palm, which will grow slowly but steadily for years to come. Repot only when really necessary.

PINEAPPLE

Here is a very attractive bromeliad that can serve in the house plant ranks for years. Cut off the top inch of the pineapple, keeping the leaves, and allow it to dry for forty-eight hours. Then plant it in a potting mixture containing plenty of sand. Maintain normal room temperatures—from 65° to 75°. Active growth will begin after an adequate root system has developed. Since the pineapple is a bromeliad, and since bromeliads take in water and nutrients through their leaves, take care to spray the plant regularly and keep its water cup (at the base of the leaves, in the center) filled with fresh water. After the plant has become well established, spray it occasionally with a fish emulsion solution to provide nutrients for vigorous growth.

COFFEE TREE

Plant a few fresh (unroasted) coffee beans in ordinary potting soil, about one-half inch deep, and give them warm temperatures. After they have germinated, select the best one or two seedlings and transplant each into a small pot. If you keep them in a shaded location in moderate temperatures, they should grow nicely. The coffee tree will flower at an early age, producing attractive white blossoms followed by red berries, which, of course, become coffee beans. One day you might be lucky enough to drink a cup of coffee brewed with beans from your own tree.

AN INDOOR VEGETABLE GARDEN

Not until the relatively recent introduction of special plant-growing fluorescent lights has it been possible to grow vegetable crops indoors with any chance of real success. Annual vegetables require moderate temperatures, good humidity, constant soil moisture, heavy fertilization, and long hours of sunlight. We have long been able to provide the first four requirements, only to be stymied by the last. Even in the sunniest south window, the amount of light received during winter's short days is inadequate for the heavy demands of annual vegetables, which must find sufficient energy to germinate, establish strong foliage, flower, then set fruit, and bring it to maturity—all in 120 days or less.

Now with special fluorescent lights that simulate the color spectrum and intensity of the sun's important rays, we can do much better than ever before, if not as well as we can outdoors during summer. Look at indoor vegetable gardening as a bold adventure with no guarantee of success. Do your best to simulate outdoor conditions, and learn by your ex-

perience. You will find some vegetables that do well, and you will grow these again and again, slowly building up your list of annual crops until you have perhaps a dozen different vegetables growing around the house at any time during winter.

The vegetables recommended here for indoor growing need sixteen hours of light a day. You can provide this best by setting up your pots and flats in a sunny south window and supplementing the window's light with a fixture holding two forty-watt plant-growing tubes attached to an automatic twenty-four-hour timer. Keep the tubes four inches above the tops of the growing plants in order to provide the strong light intensity needed. Give the plants moderately high humidity—not a steamy hothouse atmosphere but more than is found in a dry apartment. Provide good drainage, and water the plants every day, so the soil is soaked thoroughly but never allowed to puddle. Fertilize with a complete formula weekly. Spray the plants with water once a day and preferably twice. Keep the temperature at moderate levels—75° during the day, 60° at night. The exceptions will be noted below.

Almost any vegetable can be grown indoors, as long as its root requirements are not inordinately heavy or its top growth not exceptionally large. Sweet corn, broccoli, asparagus, melons, squash, okra, and similar spreading vegetables are obviously out, unless you are blessed with an enormous greenhouse. Quick-growing salad greens and radishes are relatively easy. And many other plants with requirements in between these two groups can be grown with moderate success if sufficient care is exercised. Here are some of the likely candidates for indoor vegetable growing:

CARROTS

Choose short and dwarf varieties. Thin young seedlings to one inch apart. Use the plucked seedlings in salads.

RADISHES

These are easy to grow. Thin to one inch apart. Most globe-shaped varieties are ideal for indoor growing.

BEETS

Thin plants to three inches apart after they have become established. Fertilize heavily for quick growth and tender roots.

CHINESE CABBAGE

One plant will fill an eight-inch pot. Harvest three months after planting.

PEPPERS

These are slow to grow—four months to harvest—but the foliage of the plant is so attractive that we are happy to wait. Peppers like warm temperatures and good humidity. When flowers appear, pollinate by transferring pollen from one flower to another, using an artist's soft brush, or no fruit will form.

LETTUCE

Leaf lettuce is the best bet. It likes cooler temperatures than other vegetables on this list and can be grown well under a cool basement window with supplemental light. Fertilize heavily for fast and succulent growth.

TOMATOES

These are a challenge, but they are fun to try. Choose dwarf varieties or cherry tomatoes, with one plant per twelve-inch pot. Give tomatoes the brightest window in the house, and add supplemental light for fully sixteen hours. Fertilize twice a week. The foliage will feed heavily, perhaps to the detriment of flowering and fruiting. Prune back foliage beyond the point of flowering for larger fruit. Pollinate as for peppers.

MUSHROOMS

These are ideal for dim and cool basements, but they require high humidity and good ventilation. Buy specially prepared mushroom growing kits, which contain spawn preplanted in compost, and follow the producer's directions.

CRESS

The quickest salad green known, cress is ready to harvest in two weeks. Fertilize heavily and give ample soil moisture. Plant every week for a continuous supply over the winter.

CHARD

Chard is a rewarding green and is easier to grow than lettuce. It doesn't seem to mind low humidity as much as other greens.

CORN SALAD

Another quick producer, this is also easy to grow.

SHALLOTS

For the gourmet in you, plant shallots in sandy soil, and give ample moisture and fertilizer.

SEED SPROUTS

The seeds of many plants may be sprouted in a few days and then used in salads, stews, and many recipes. Buy untreated seeds from a health food store. Soak them overnight, drain, and spread out in a shallow container. Cover with a double layer of cheesecloth, and put in a warm place. Rinse and drain the seeds three times a day; they will be ready to eat in three to five days, when they have sprouted. Almost any seeds can be sprouted, although the best include barley, alfalfa, soybeans, lentils, mung beans, rye, millet, and wheat.

HERBS

A wide variety of herbs may be grown indoors, some in sunny windows with no supplemental light. Most have attractive foliage and so make good decorative plants as well. Many are suitable for hanging baskets. All but the largest of herbs, such as dill, caraway, and fennel, are indoor candidates. The list includes chives, mint, parsley, rosemary, sage, sweet basil, thyme, and winter savory. Many herbs raised outdoors may be potted, cut back, and brought indoors in the autumn.

 Plant Troubles and Cures

Your indoor plants stand a far better chance of avoiding insect and disease attack than those plants that live outdoors. For one thing, the leaf surfaces of house plants are most often dry, meaning that a host of harmful fungi and viruses—which commonly attack outdoor plants—will never bother your indoor green guests. Then, unless you do not use window screens, the chances of insects entering the home to nest in house plants are reasonably slim. Your house plants, merely by being indoors, are offered a high degree of protection.

Still, occasional problems present themselves, interfering with the health and good appearance of plants. The troubles may be divided into three broad areas—insects, diseases, and improper handling. We will approach the last of these first, since improper handling and care are likely to be the cause of many common troubles.

IMPROPER HANDLING AND CARE

Overwatering is by far the most common cause of plant problems. Too much water impedes air exchange in the soil, excluding the oxygen that is vital to plant health. If your plants' leaves begin to lose color and drop (usually starting at the base and proceeding upward along the stalk), look first to your watering habits. Overwatering also can cause leaves to spot, and continual overwatering can cause root rot and the eventual loss of the offended plant.

Underwatering, on the other hand, can cause wilt and stunted growth. If you have neglected watering to the point of your plant's wilting, submerge the pot immediately in water of room temperature, until the soil is thoroughly moistened, and spray the foliage thoroughly. The plant should be revived by the following day.

Shock can also cause drastic changes in a plant's health. Leaves can change color and fall if the plant meets a sudden and severe temperature change or a sudden change in daily light received. Cold drafts will result in a browning of the tips of leaves, although this condition can also be caused by overfertilizing, insect attack, or improper watering. The shock of transplanting is usually overcome within several days and can be meliorated by your following the rules carefully.

A lack of fertilizer can gradually lead to a loss of normal leaf color and a generally unhealthy appearance of the plant. Again, though, it is better to underfertilize than to overfertilize.

Spots on the leaves may also result from the spraying of a plant while it is standing in direct sunlight. The little droplets on the leaves act as magnifying lenses, causing burn spots. Spots may also be caused by spraying leaves with overconcentrated pesticides or by insect attack.

INSECT FOES

Many house plant growers can go along for years with nary an insect problem. The atmosphere of a normal home is, first, often unconducive to insect breeding, so any insects that do enter the home quickly die out. Second, most of us insulate our homes carefully against winged, crawling, and creeping intruders, and our indoor plants should rest assured in our protection.

Yet there are times when insects do attack—and in some

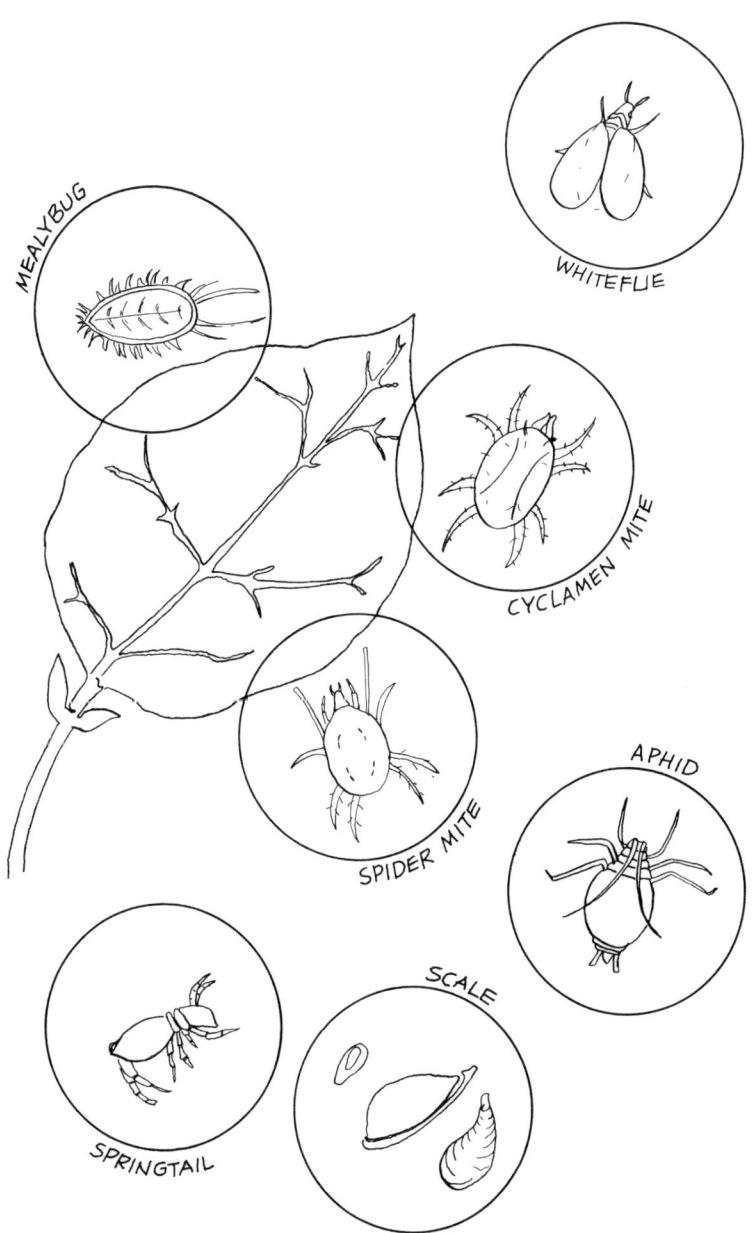

MEALYBUG

WHITEFLIE

CYCLAMEN MITE

SPIDER MITE

APHID

SPRINGTAIL

SCALE

instances, the infestation of one plant can rapidly spread to all household plants, creating a problem of massive proportions. It will be wise for you to learn to recognize the symptoms of insect attack and to guard against them.

One common-sense rule is to isolate all newcomers for at least one week and preferably two. If you bring plants indoors after a summer vacation outdoors, inspect them carefully with the aid of a hand lens, and then place them in a separate room of the house, keeping the door closed. Inspect the plants several times during the isolation period for signs of attack. If none appears after two weeks, you may be fairly certain that no harmful insects are being harbored nor diseases spread. Only then should you return the plants to the greater community.

House plants can be injured by many different kinds of insects, some of which thrive only in isolated sections of the country. Here we will concentrate only on the most common offenders, those which claim most of the nation as their territory and which are most likely to make themselves thoroughly disliked by you.

Spider Mites

Spider mites, or red spiders, are among the most virulent attackers of house plants. They thrive in the warm, dry atmosphere of your home and will readily take up residence among your prize plants. Spider mites are almost too small to be seen with the naked eye. Small white spots on plant leaves may be evidence of spider mite activity, the result of the mites having sucked juices from the leaf surface. If the infestation is sizable, leaves will gradually take on a fine webbed appearance, have a vaguely fuzzy feeling on their undersides, and eventually feel crumbly. The attack if unchecked can prove fatal.

Since spider mites thrive on warmth and dryness, control rests on making them cold and wet. At least in the early stages they can be eliminated by washing the plant with a mild soap (not detergent) solution and then spraying the entire plant vigorously with cold water, being sure to hit the undersides of leaves where the mites are usually harbored. Repeat this process weekly until the infestation has ceased. In the meantime spray plants daily with a fine mist, preferably in the morning, again being sure to reach the undersides of leaves. If the infestation is truly severe, a solution of rotenone and/or pyrethrum may be used. Both are of low toxicity to warm-blooded creatures, including children, dogs, and cats, although rotenone is very toxic to fish. More potent chemicals, not for organic gardeners, are malathion and kelthane.

Mealybugs

Mealybugs concentrate on the undersides of leaves, at stem joints, and along leaf veins to cause the stunting of plants by sucking their juices. They can be detected easily, since the adult is about one-fourth inch long, and the young are contained in small cottony cases. The egg cases may be destroyed by wiping them off with a cotton swab dipped in rubbing alcohol. Try to avoid alcohol contact with the plant, however, and rinse the plant thoroughly afterward. Adult mealybugs may be combatted with the same methods as recommended for the control of spider mites. Mealybugs sometimes infest the roots of plants, also, causing stunting and general ill health of foliage. In cases of heavy root infestation, it is best to take a few cuttings, inspect them carefully for infestation, start new plants, and discard the old plant, taking care to scald the pot and scrub it thoroughly before putting it back into service. Discard the old soil.

Cyclamen Mites

Cyclamen mites are most often a danger to African violets, begonias, *Cissus*, cyclamen, English ivy, *Episcia*, geraniums, and gloxinias. These minute creatures can cause leaves to darken and curl and can stunt the plant. They prefer to attack soft and growing shoots and buds, causing the latter to drop or be deformed. Cyclamen mites are devilish to combat, because they congregate in plant parts that are difficult to reach. Furthermore, they can be transmitted from one plant to another with alarming ease, simply by your touching one plant and then another. For control, again use the methods recommended for spider mite control. House plant expert Raymond P. Poincelot recommends, as a last resort, immersing the entire plant for fifteen minutes in water heated to 110°.* The usual recommended chemical is dicofol, but even this is effective only if sprayed directly into the areas where the mites are congregated.

Springtails

Springtails, or *Collembola*, range in size from microscopic to one-fifth inch in length. They live on or near the soil surface and can readily be seen jumping about when the plant is watered from the top. They will often feed on the tender parts of plants. Rotenone and/or pyrethrum will control springtails easily.

Whiteflies

Whiteflies are treacherous, largely because they can fly from plant to plant. The infestation of one plant, therefore, can result very quickly in the attack upon all. The adults are, as their name implies, white in color, about one-sixteenth inch long. They usually can be seen when the plant is disturbed, for they will dart about in the air, together resembling a snow flurry. Like most insect pests, they suck the juices from leaves, causing them to shrivel, to turn yellow, and eventually to drop. The first measure to adopt is complete isolation of the infested plant in order to protect others in the green community. Wash the plant immediately in a mild soap solution; then rinse it thoroughly, allow the foliage to dry, and finally spray with rotenone and/or pyrethrum. Chemical gardeners use an aerosol spray containing malathion or thiodan.

*Raymond P. Poincelot, *Gardening Indoors with House Plants*, Emmaus, Pa., Rodale Press, 1974, p. 52.

Aphids

Aphids *(aphis,* or plant lice*)* are tiny insects, ranging in color from green to black, that cluster on the undersides of leaves, on stems, or on roots. They suck the sap of the plant, causing distorted leaves and eventually stunted plants. Aphids can be washed off plants with a strong stream of water. Tobacco sprinkled on top of the potting mixture seems to repel them. In cases of large-scale infestation, chemical gardeners use malathion.

Scale

Like aphids, scale insects are tiny creatures that cluster on leaves and stems, suck the sap from the plant, and eventually cause its parts to become distorted and stunted. Scale can be removed easily by a strong stream of water, by wiping the plants with a cotton swab dipped in alcohol or by washing with a strong soap solution. Chemical gardeners use Black Leaf 40 or a wide-spectrum house plant aerosol.

The foregoing are some of the most common of insect pests. Others are thrips, fungus gnats, symphylids, nematodes, and a few that confine themselves to the Deep South. Nearly all can be controlled by general preventive measures first and, in cases of actual attack, by adopting the general measures recommended for spider mite control. If you wish to obtain more detailed information about the subject, I suggest that you obtain a copy of the United States Department of Agriculture Home and Garden Bulletin 67, *Insects and Related Pests of House Plants,* available from your county agricultural agent or from the USDA, Washington, D.C. 20250. One very good book on organic methods is *Organic Plant Protection,* available at many bookstores or from the publisher, Rodale Press, Inc., Emmaus, Pa. 18049. It covers both indoor and outdoor plants in great detail.

DISEASES

Diseases—caused either by fungi, bacteria, or viruses—are

unlikely to cause serious problems for your house plants. Many fungi and bacteria need cool and constantly damp surfaces in order to become established, and these conditions simply will not be offered by the normal home environment.

Still there always exists the possibility of disease, and you should be aware of that possibility and be prepared to meet the problem. The diseases most likely to affect house plants are *Botrytis*, crown and root rot, damping-off, leaf spot, powdery mildew, rusts, and various viral infections. The symptoms vary, although all will cause a general lack of vigor, a dull appearance, and stunted growth of the plant. *Botrytis* causes a fuzzy gray mold, while powdery mildew leaves a gray white powdery mold on leaves and stems. Rusts leave red or brown spots on leaves. Not all of these are serious, except those that attack roots and crowns of plants and the virus diseases for which there are no cures.

Against disease organisms the best offense is a good defense. Create the conditions for your house plants that will lessen the chances of disease attack. These include all the advice on proper handling and care that has been offered in preceding pages. Especially avoid continuing cool and damp conditions, overcrowding, overwatering, and lack of ventilation.

Damping-off is a particularly pernicious disease that can wipe out hundreds—or thousands—of young seedlings overnight. The disease attacks plants at the soil line and simply mows them down dead. It can be prevented by using a sterile rooting medium. Many growers spread about one-fourth inch of sterile sand on top of the regular starting medium; damping-off cannot exist on sterile sand. Other prevention methods include moderate and proper watering of seedlings, proper ventilation, and prompt thinning.

Sanitation is crucially important in disease prevention. Since organisms are spread easily through air movement, by the transfer of soil, and by your hands, take extra precautions whenever you suspect the presence of a plant disease. Wash your hands thoroughly after handling a diseased plant or any newcomer. Sterilize garden soil before using it

for house plants (an hour, spread out on a tray, in a medium oven will do the trick), and boil for fifteen minutes any pot which has contained a diseased plant. Last, never reuse soil that has supported a diseased plant.

If a disease does threaten your plants seriously, you may have it identified by taking an affected plant to a plant pathologist at your state university or asking your county agricultural agent for advice on seeking positive identification. If you would prefer to mail the plant for analysis, call your county agent for precise instructions. In the meantime isolate all affected plants for the duration of the illness and take cuttings immediately from any favorite plants.

The last word on insect and disease control is one of ruthlessness. If a plant is affected severely, it is often best simply to throw it out, pot and all. You have no time to spend in nursing sick plants back to health, and (unless such activity satisfies a need deep within you) you will be happier in getting rid of the sick plant and buying a new one.

Appendix

PLANTS FOR COOL TEMPERATURES
(50°–60° AT NIGHT)

Aloe
Aspidistra
Australian laurel
Azalea
Baby's tears
Black pepper
Boxwood
Bromeliads
Cacti
Calceolaria
Camellia
Cape ivy
Christmas begonia
Chrysanthemum
Cineraria
Citrus
Creeping fig
Cyclamen
Easter lily
English ivy

Fatshedra
Fiddleleaf fig
Flowering maple
Freesia
Fuchsia
Geranium
German ivy
Honeysuckle
Hyacinth
Jasmine
Jerusalem cherry
Kalanchoe
Kangaroo vine
Lily-of-the-valley
Lithops
Miniature holly
Mother of thousands
Narcissus
Oxalis
Primrose

Sensitive plant

Silk oak

Snake plant

Spindletree

Tulip

Vinca

Wandering Jew

White calla lily

PLANTS FOR MEDIUM TEMPERATURES
(60°–65° AT NIGHT)

Achimenes

Aechmea

Amaryllis

Ardisia

Asparagus fern

Aspidistra

Avocado

Begonia

Bird's-nest fern

Browallia

Chenille plant

Christmas cactus

Chrysanthemum

Citrus

Coleus

Copper leaf

Crown of thorns

Cryptanthus

Dracaena

Easter lily

Echeveria

English ivy

Gardenia

Grape ivy

Hibiscus

Hydrangea

Maranta

Norfolk Island pine

Palms

Peperomia

Philodendron scandens

Pilea

Poinsettia

Rubber plant

Shrimp plant

Silk oak

Snake plant

Staghorn fern

Ti plant

Tuberous begonia

Umbrella tree

Velvet plant

Wax begonia

Wax plant

Weeping fig

Yellow calla lily

PLANTS FOR HIGH TEMPERATURES
(65°–75° AT NIGHT)

African violet

Aphelandra

Arrowhead

Banded maranta

Cacti and succulents

Caladium

Chinese evergreen
Cocos palm
Croton
Dieffenbachia
Dracaena
Episcia
False aralia
Fiddleleaf fig
Gloxinia
Gold-dust plant

Goosefoot plant
Mistletoe fig
Philodendron
Pothos *(Scindapsus)*
Seersucker plant
Snake plant
Spathiphyllum
Umbrella tree
Veitch screw pine
Zebra plant

PLANTS FOR DRY AND SEMIDRY CONDITIONS

Aloe
Aspidistra
Bromeliads
Cacti
Cape ivy
Coleus
Crown of thorns
Dracaena marginata
Echeveria
Fatshedra japonica
Fatsia lizei

Hedera (ivy)
Kalanchoe
Lithops
Norfolk Island pine
Oval-leaf peperomia
Pothos *(Scindapsus)*
Snake plant
Spider plant
Wandering Jew
Wax flower

VINES AND TRAILING PLANTS FOR TOTEM POLES

Arrowhead
Black pepper
Canary Islands ivy
Creeping fig
English ivy
Grape ivy
Kangaroo vine

Pellionia
Philodendron
Pothos (Scindapsus)
Syngonium
Velvet plant
Wax plant

PLANTS FOR HANGING BASKETS

African violet
Artillery plant
Asparagus fern
Baby's tears
Begonia (some types)
Black pepper
Creeping fig
English ivy
Episcia
Fuchsia (some types)
German ivy
Goldfish plant
Grape ivy

Honeysuckle
Italian bellflower
Ivy geranium
Peperomia (some types)
Philodendron (some types)
Pothos *(Scindapsus)*
Saxifraga
Spider plant
Syngonium
Trailing coleus
Wandering Jew
Wax plant

PLANTS FOR LARGE TUBS

Dracaena
False aralia
Fatshedra
Fiddleleaf fig
Norfolk Island pine
Palm
Philodendron (some types)

Rubber plant
Silk oak
Tuftroot
Umbrella tree
Veitch screw pine
Weeping fig

Bibliography

ARTIFICIAL LIGHT GARDENING

Bickford, Elwood D., and Stuart Dunn. *Lighting for Plant Growth.* Kent, Ohio, Kent State University Press, 1972. One of the best books on the subject; especially valuable to those who have had some experience in the area.

Cherry, Elaine C. *Fluorescent Light Gardening.* New York, Van Nostrand Reinhold Co., 1965.

Elbert, George A. *The Indoor Light Gardening Book.* New York, Crown Publishers, 1975.

Fitch, Charles Marden. *The Complete Book of Houseplants under Lights.* New York, Hawthorn Books, 1975.

Kranz, Frederick H., and Jacqueline Kranz. *Gardening Indoors under Lights.* New York, Viking Press, rev. 1971.

BEGONIAS

Brilmayer, Bernice. *All About Begonias.* New York, Doubleday Publishing Co., 1960.

Kramer, Jack. *Begonias, Indoors and Out.* New York, E. P. Dutton & Co., 1967.

BONSAI

Brooklyn Botanic Garden. *Bonsai: Special Techniques.* New York,

132

Brooklyn Botanic Garden.

Chidamian, Claude. *Bonsai: Miniature Trees.* New York, Van Nostrand Reinhold Co., 1955.

BROMELIADS

Kramer, Jack. *Bromeliads: The Colorful House Plants.* New York, Van Nostrand Reinhold Co., 1965.

BULBS

Field, Xenia. *Growing Bulbs in the House.* New York, St. Martin's Press, 1966.

Peters, Ruth Marie. *Bulb Magic in Your Window.* New York, M. Barrows & Co., 1954.

Walker, Marion C. *Flowering Bulbs for Winter Windows.* New York, Van Nostrand Reinhold Co., 1965.

CACTI AND OTHER SUCCULENTS

Britton, W. L., and J. N. Rose. *The Cactaceae.* New York, Dover Publications, rpt. 1973. A reprinted classic of the Carnegie Institution (1937). Comprehensive.

Brooklyn Botanic Garden. *Handbook on Succulent Plants.* New York, Brooklyn Botanic Garden, 1970.

Cutak, Ladislaus. *Cactus Guide.* New York, Van Nostrand Reinhold Co., 1956.

FERNS AND PALMS

Kramer, Jack. *Ferns and Palms for Interior Decoration.* New York, Charles Scribner's Sons, 1972.

FLOWERING HOUSE PLANTS

Crockett, James Underwood. *Flowering House Plants.* New York, Time-Life Books, 1971.

133

FOLIAGE HOUSE PLANTS

Crockett, James Underwood. *Foliage House Plants*. New York, Time-Life Books, 1972.

GENERAL AND REFERENCE WORKS

Bechtel, Helmut. *House Plant Identifier*. New York, Sterling Publishing Co., 1973.

Dworkin, Florence, and Stanley Dworkin. *The Apartment Gardener*. New York, The New American Library, 1974.

Faust, Joan Lee. *The New York Times Book of House Plants*. New York, Quadrangle/The New York Times Book Co., 1973.

Kramer, Jack. *The Indoor Gardener's How-to-Build-It Book*. New York, Simon & Schuster, 1974.

McDonald, Elvin. *House Plants to Grow If You Have No Sun*. New York, Popular Library, 1975.

————. *The World Book of House Plants*. New York, Popular Library, 1963.

Mott, Russell C. *The Total Book of House Plants*. New York, Delacorte Press, 1975.

Poincelot, Raymond P. *Gardening Indoors with House Plants*. Emmaus, Pa., Rodale Press, 1974. A complete indoor guide for the organic gardener.

Tenenbaum, Frances. *Plants from 9:00 to 5:00: Gardening Where You Work*. New York, Charles Scribner's Sons, 1977.

Wright, Michael, ed. *The Complete Indoor Gardener*. New York, Random House, 1974. Hundreds of color photographs highlight this handsome, large-format paperback edition.

GERANIUMS

Schulz, Peggie. *All About Geraniums*. New York, Doubleday Publishing Co., 1965.

Wilson, Helen Van Pelt. *The Joy of Geraniums*. New York, M. Barrows & Co., 1967.

GESNERIADS

Brooklyn Botanic Garden: *Handbook on Gesneriads.* New York, Brooklyn Botanic Garden, 1967.

Elbert, Virginie F., and George A. Elbert. *Miracle Houseplants: The Gesneriad Family.* New York, Crown Publishers, 1976.

Moore, Harold E., Jr. *African Violets, Gloxinias, and Their Relatives.* New York, The Macmillan Co., 1957.

Schulz, Peggie, ed. *Gesneriads and How to Grow Them.* Kansas City, Mo., Diversity Books, 1967.

Schulz, Peggie. *Gloxinias and How to Grow Them.* New York, M. Barrows & Co., 1965.

Wilson, Helen Van Pelt. *New Complete Book of African Violets.* New York, M. Barrows & Co., rev. 1963.

HANGING GARDENS

Baumgardt, John Philip. *Hanging Plants for Home, Terrace, and Garden.* New York, Simon & Schuster, 1972.

Brilmayer, Bernice. *All About Vines and Hanging Plants.* New York, Doubleday Publishing Co., 1962.

Kramer, Jack. *Hanging Gardens.* New York, Charles Scribner's Sons, 1973.

HERBS AND VEGETABLES

Elbert, Virginie F., and George A. Elbert. *Fun with Growing Herbs Indoors.* New York, Crown Publishers, 1974.

Meschter, Joan W. *How to Grow Herbs and Salad Greens Indoors.* New York, Popular Library, 1975.

Skelsey, Alice. *Farming in a Flowerpot.* New York, Workman Publishing Co., 1971.

KITCHEN SCRAP GARDENS

Canaday, John. *The Artful Avocado.* New York, Doubleday Publishing Co., 1973. About avocados exclusively.

135

Kramer, Jack. *The Pit 'n' Pot Grower's Book.* New York, Thomas Y. Crowell Co., 1975.

MINIATURE GARDENS AND PLANTS

Kramer, Jack. *Miniature Gardens in Bowl, Dish and Tray.* New York, Charles Scribner's Sons, 1975.

McDonald, Elvin. *Miniature Plants for Home and Greenhouse.* New York, Van Nostrand Reinhold Co., 1962.

PROPAGATING, PRUNING, AND PLANT CARE

Ballard, Ernesta Drinker. *The Art of Training Plants.* New York, Barnes & Noble Books, 1962.

Evans, Charles M. *New Plants from Old: Pruning and Propagating for the Indoor Gardener.* New York, Random House, 1976.

Evans, Charles M., and Roberta Lee Pliner. *Rx for Ailing House Plants.* New York, Random House, 1974. Diagnosing and treating plant ills.

Loewer, H. Peter. *The Indoor Gardener's Guide to Seeds and Cuttings.* New York, Walker & Co., 1975.

Nehrling, Arno, and Irene Arno. *Propagating House Plants.* Great Neck, N.Y., Hearthside Press, 1971.

TERRARIUMS AND BOTTLE GARDENS

Baur, Robert. *Gardens in Glass Containers.* Great Neck, N.Y., Hearthside Press, 1970.

Elbert, Virginie F., and George A. Elbert. *Fun with Terrarium Gardening.* New York, Crown Publishers, 1973.

Evans, Charles M., and Roberta Lee Pliner. *The Terrarium Book.* New York, Random House, 1973.

TREE-TYPE PLANTS

Kramer, Jack. *Indoor Trees.* New York, Hawthorne Books, Inc., 1975.

Subject Index

Index of Plant Names